30-MINUTE AIR FRYER COOKBOOK FOR BEGINNERS

PLUNGE INTO QUICK, NUTRITIOUS AND TASTY DISHES
|THE ULTIMATE AIR FRYER EXPERTISE GUIDE|

FIRST EDITION: JANUARY 2024

© Copyright 2024 by Anastasia Wilson- All rights reserved.

The following book is reproduced below to provide information that is as accurate and reliable as possible. Regardless, purchasing this book can be seen as consent because both the publisher and the author of this book are in no way experts on the topics discussed within. Any recommendations or suggestions that are made herein are for entertainment purposes only. Professionals should be consulted as needed before undertaking any of the actions endorsed herein. This declaration is deemed fair and valid by both the American Bar Association and the Committee of Publishers Association and is legally binding throughout the United States. Furthermore, the transmission, duplication, or reproduction of any of the following work, including specific information, will be considered an illegal act irrespective of if it is done electronically or in print. This extends to creating a secondary or tertiary copy of the work or a recorded document and is only allowed to express written consent from the publisher. All additional rights reserved. The information in the following pages is broadly considered a truthful and accurate account of facts. As such, any inattention, use, or misuse of the information in question by the reader will render any resulting actions solely under their purview. There are no scenarios in which the publisher or the original author of this work can be in any fashion deemed liable for any hardship or damages that may befall them after undertaking the information described herein. Additionally, the following pages' information is intended only for informational purposes and should thus be thought of as universal. As befitting its nature, it is presented without assurance regarding its prolonged validity or interim quality. Trademarks that are mentioned are done without written consent and can in no way be considered an endorsement from the trademark holder.

Thank You For Your Support!

★★★★★

I'm eager to know what you think!

Simply **scan this QR code** to jump straight to my book's review page on Amazon.

Your insights are invaluable – they aid in my growth as an author and assist others in discovering this cookbook.

Feel free to **share a photo or video review showcasing a recipe** you tried. Your experience could inspire others to embark on their culinary adventure with my book!

Anastasia

Introduction

1. Why Air Fry?

A Brief History of The Air Fryer

The air fryer, a groundbreaking kitchen device, has its origins in the pursuit of healthier cooking techniques. Although the concept of utilizing circulating hot air for cooking has historical roots in the convection oven, the familiar air fryer we know today emerged in the early 2010s in the consumer market. Philips, a Dutch company, is acknowledged for introducing the initial domestic air fryer in 2010. Their aim was to provide individuals with the enjoyment of fried food flavors and textures without the excessive use of oil and the associated health hazards. The technology underlying the air fryer incorporates a robust fan that circulates superheated air around the food, resulting in a crispy exterior akin to deep frying but with significantly less oil. This inventive approach garnered widespread enthusiasm, particularly within health-conscious communities. Over time, the air fryer has gained immense popularity, prompting developments in design, capacity, and additional features. Originating in Europe, the air fryer swiftly transcended continents, establishing itself as a cherished kitchen essential in households worldwide. Its swift rise in the culinary realm underscores the global demand for healthier eating without compromising on taste and texture.

Benefits Of Air Frying (Health, Convenience, Versatility)

Air frying has swiftly gained popularity among both culinary enthusiasts and health-conscious individuals, and the reasons are compelling. A key advantage lies in its positive impact on health. Unlike traditional frying methods that immerse food in oil, resulting in elevated fat levels, air frying requires minimal to no oil. This leads to dishes with significantly reduced fat and calorie content, enabling individuals to enjoy their favorite fried foods without guilt or health worries. In addition to health benefits, air fryers offer unparalleled convenience. With shorter cooking times compared to conventional ovens and the absence of the messy aftermath associated with deep frying, they prove to be time-efficient in today's fast-paced world. No more waiting for oil to heat up or dealing with splatters and spills – simply place your ingredients in the air fryer, set the timer, and let the machine do its work. Lastly, the versatility of air fryers is truly noteworthy. Going beyond mere "frying," these appliances can also roast, grill, bake, and even dehydrate. Whether the craving is for crispy fries, a succulent steak, or a piece of cake, the air fryer can handle it all. This adaptability makes it a valuable addition to any kitchen, meeting a wide range of culinary preferences and needs. In summary, the air fryer combines health, convenience, and versatility, reshaping modern cooking practices.

2. Getting Started with Your Air Fryer

Understanding Your Air Fryer's Components and Functions

The air fryer, though compact in its design, stands as an engineering marvel, incorporating several essential components working in tandem to achieve the perfect fry. At its core lies the cooking chamber, where the culinary magic unfolds. Emitting heat from a nearby heating element, this chamber produces a crispy layer reminiscent of traditional frying. Positioned above the chamber is a robust fan that circulates hot air around the food, ensuring uniform cooking and that sought-after crispy texture.

Situated at the chamber's base is typically a pull-out drawer housing a perforated basket. This specific design facilitates the drainage of excess fat from the food, enhancing the health benefits associated with air frying. On the exterior, a control panel is commonly found, varying from simple dials to advanced digital touchscreens. Users can set the temperature and cooking duration here and, in more sophisticated models, choose from an array of preset cooking functions. Some air fryers even incorporate additional features like rotisserie spits or racks for layering food.

A comprehensive understanding of these components is imperative for optimal utilization. For example, ensuring the unobstructed nature of the basket's perforations can enhance air circulation, and familiarity with the control panel can unlock a plethora of culinary possibilities. Essentially, while the air fryer may appear uncomplicated, a deeper comprehension of its components and functions has the potential to elevate the overall cooking experience.

Basic Setup and Safety Tips

Setting up your air fryer is typically uncomplicated, but adhering to some fundamental guidelines is essential to ensure both optimal performance and safety. Firstly, place your air fryer on a flat, stable surface, ensuring it maintains a distance from walls or other appliances, as it emits heat during operation. Before the initial use, wash all removable components with warm, soapy water to eliminate any manufacturing residues. When using the air fryer, securely position the cooking basket to prevent accidents. While the device is running, avoid blocking the exhaust vent, which releases hot air. Overfilling the basket can result in uneven cooking and potential smoking.

Regularly check on food to prevent overcooking, and after each use, unplug the air fryer, allowing it to cool before cleaning or storing. Refrain from using metal utensils that could scratch the non-stick surface of the cooking basket. Exercise caution when opening the basket after cooking, as the released steam can be extremely hot. By adhering to these basic setup and safety guidelines, you can savor delicious meals while ensuring the longevity of your air fryer and prioritizing safety.

3. Tips for Perfect Air Frying Every Time

Preheating, Shaking, And Flipping

Mastering preheating, shaking, and flipping techniques are crucial for achieving optimal results with your air fryer. Similar to a traditional oven, preheating ensures that the cooking chamber attains the desired temperature, ensuring consistent cooking from the moment your food is placed inside. Often overlooked, this step can be the key to achieving a perfectly crispy exterior rather than a lackluster result.

Shaking is particularly important for smaller food items such as fries or vegetable cuts. A gentle shake midway through the cooking process ensures that hot air circulates around each piece, promoting even browning and preventing pieces from sticking together. For larger items like chicken breasts or patties, flipping serves a similar purpose. Turning the food over guarantees equal exposure to the intense heat, resulting in a uniformly cooked and crispy outcome.

These simple yet effective techniques, when applied correctly, enhance the quality of dishes produced in an air fryer, bringing them closer to the deep-fried favorites we love but with significantly less oil and calories.

Importance Of Not Overcrowding

One fundamental guideline to follow when using an air fryer is to avoid overcrowding the cooking basket. The air fryer's effectiveness lies in its capacity to circulate hot air around the food, ensuring even cooking and achieving the desired crispy texture. Overcrowding hinders this air circulation, resulting in unevenly cooked dishes and a compromise in crispiness. When food items are stacked on top of each other, the surfaces in contact do not receive sufficient exposure to the hot air, leading to patches that are either undercooked or soggy. Additionally, overcrowding can prolong cooking time, as the heat struggles to penetrate the dense pile of food. For optimal outcomes, it is recommended to cook in batches, providing each piece with ample space to guarantee maximum air circulation. This straightforward consideration ensures that every bite is perfectly cooked and delightfully crispy.

Using Oil and Alternatives

While the air fryer's primary allure is its capacity to cook with minimal oil, a light application of oil can enhance the texture and flavor of specific dishes. A subtle mist of oil can elevate the crispiness of foods, replicating the desired deep-fried texture. However, it's crucial to use oil sparingly; an excessive amount can result in sogginess and smoke. For those prioritizing healthier options, cooking sprays or oil mists are excellent alternatives, offering a thin, even layer without unnecessary excess.

Moreover, certain foods release their natural fats during cooking, eliminating the necessity for additional oil. For individuals mindful of their health, alternatives such as broths or citrus juice can serve as substitutes for marinating or basting foods, imparting moisture and flavor without introducing extra fat. By experimenting with oils and their alternatives, one can achieve the desired taste and texture while upholding health considerations.

4. Adapting Traditional Recipes for the Air Fryer

Adjusting Cooking Times and Temperatures

Mastering the intricacies of cooking times and temperatures is essential to fully utilizing your air fryer. Although renowned for their speed and efficiency, air fryers operate differently than traditional ovens and stovetops. Recipes designed for conventional ovens often require modifications when adapted to an air fryer. Generally, it's advisable to decrease the cooking temperature by approximately 25°F (or 15°C) compared to oven. This modification accounts for the intense heat circulation in the air fryer, thus preventing food from burning or drying out.

In addition to temperature adjustments, it's common for cooking times to be shortened. Foods cooked in an air fryer typically require 20-25% less time, prompting the need to check for doneness earlier than suggested in the original recipe. However, these adjustments aren't universally applicable. Variables such as the size of the food, the specific air fryer model, and individual taste preferences can influence the optimal time and temperature. Starting conservatively, monitoring the cooking process, and making adjustments as necessary are prudent practices to ensure consistently well-cooked dishes.

Considering The Size and Capacity of The Air Fryer

The size and capacity of an air fryer are critical factors that significantly impact the success of your cooking endeavors. Air fryers are available in various sizes, ranging from compact models suitable for individuals or couples to larger units designed for family use. It is crucial to understand the capacity of your device to ensure even cooking and to avoid overcrowding.

Smaller air fryers may necessitate cooking in batches, especially when preparing meals for multiple people, while larger ones can accommodate larger portions or multiple food items simultaneously. However, even with ample space, it is essential to resist the temptation to overfill the air fryer. Ensuring sufficient room for hot air to circulate freely around each food item is essential for achieving the desired crispy finish.

Furthermore, the size of the air fryer can impact cooking times. A compact model may cook faster due to the proximity of the food to the heating element, while a larger one might require slight adjustments. By being mindful of your air fryer's size and capacity and adjusting recipes accordingly, you can consistently achieve delicious and perfectly cooked results.

5. Meal Planning with the Air Fryer

How To Incorporate Air Fryer Recipes into Weekly Meal Plans

Integrating air fryer recipes into your weekly meal plans can revolutionize your approach to efficiency without compromising on taste. The air fryer's versatility extends to handling breakfasts, lunches, dinners, and even snacks. Kickstart your week by identifying the meals you intend to prepare. For breakfast, explore options like air-fried granola or quick pastries. Lunches can range from simply reheating leftovers to preserve their crispiness to crafting gourmet sandwiches. Dinners open up a myriad of possibilities, spanning from crispy tofu bites to succulent chicken drumsticks.

Once your meals are outlined, create a comprehensive shopping list to ensure you have all the necessary ingredients readily available. Considering batch cooking is another effective strategy. By preparing larger quantities of a particular dish and reheating portions throughout the week, you can save time and alleviate daily cooking stress, and the air fryer's ability to re-crisp foods makes it well-suited for this approach.

These practices ensure you are maximizing the potential of your appliance. Thoughtfully integrating air fryer recipes into your weekly routine allows you to streamline your meal preparation while relishing a diverse array of delicious dishes.

Batch Cooking and Reheating

The concept of batch cooking, involving the preparation of larger quantities of food for future consumption, aligns seamlessly with the capabilities of the air fryer. This approach not only saves time on hectic weekdays but also guarantees consistent meal quality. The design of the air fryer excels in reheating batch-cooked foods, restoring their initial crispiness and flavor without the sogginess often associated with microwaving.

For example, over the weekend, one can cook a batch of homemade chicken wings or vegetable fritters, store them in the refrigerator, and quickly reheat them in the air fryer for a midweek meal. The circulating hot air rejuvenates the food's texture, providing a taste reminiscent of freshly cooked meals. The synergy between batch cooking and the air fryer's reheating capabilities presents a practical solution for those who wish to enjoy homemade meals with minimal daily cooking effort.

6. Cleaning and Maintenance

Best Practices for Cleaning After Each Use

Maintaining the cleanliness of your air fryer is crucial, not only for the appliance's longevity but also for ensuring the quality and safety of the food it prepares. After each use, it's imperative to conduct a thorough cleaning to prevent residue build-up and potential hazards like smoke or fire. To initiate the cleaning process, unplug the device and let it cool completely. Remove the cooking basket and pan, and wash them with warm soapy water. Since most baskets are non-stick, it's advisable to use a soft sponge or cloth to prevent any scratches. For stubborn food residues, soaking the components for a few minutes can facilitate easier removal. Wipe down the interior of the air fryer with a damp cloth to eliminate any grease or food particles.

It's crucial to ensure that all components are completely dry before reassembly to prevent the growth of mold or bacteria. The exterior of the air fryer can be cleaned with a damp cloth and then dried. Regular cleaning not only guarantees optimal performance but also extends the lifespan of your air fryer, making it a worthwhile investment in both time and effort.

Maintaining Your Air Fryer for Longevity

Ensuring the prolonged functionality and efficiency of your air fryer extends beyond routine cleaning; it necessitates a comprehensive maintenance approach. First and foremost, it is crucial to consult the user manual specific to your model, as manufacturers often provide tailored guidelines and tips to maintain the appliance in optimal condition.

When utilizing the air fryer, ensure it is positioned in a well-ventilated location to prevent overheating. After each use, inspect the heating element for any food residues or debris, as these can lead to smoke or even fire in subsequent uses. Periodically examine the electrical cord and plug for any signs of wear or damage, and if irregularities are detected, consider repairing or replacing the unit for safety. Store your air fryer in a dry, cool place, away from direct sunlight or extreme temperatures. If your model includes a removable air filter, ensure it is cleaned or replaced according to the manufacturer's recommendations.

Lastly, refrain from using metal utensils or abrasive cleaning agents, as these can damage the non-stick surface of the cooking basket. By adopting these maintenance practices, you can ensure that your air fryer remains a dependable kitchen companion for years to come.

7. Let's Get Cooking!

The Variety of Recipes in The Book (Starters, First Courses, Main Courses)

This cookbook is a culinary treasure trove crafted to cater to diverse palates and various meal occasions. It begins with an enticing assortment of starters and appetizers, setting the stage for the gastronomic journey ahead. These bite-sized delights are ideal for social gatherings or as a prelude to a main meal. Moving on to the first courses, the book presents a variety of heartier dishes suitable for a light lunch or dinner, showcasing the air fryer's versatility in handling diverse ingredients and cuisines.

The main courses section stands out as the pièce de résistance, offering a multitude of dishes that both satiate and satisfy. Whether it's succulent chicken roasts for meat enthusiasts or flavorful vegetable dishes for vegetarians and vegans, there is something to appeal to every palate. Collectively, these sections underscore the book's dedication to providing a comprehensive air frying experience.

STARTERS

ROASTED PEPPER CROSTINI

Servings: 2 people
Difficulty: Easy
Cooking Time: 26 minutes

Ingredients:
- 3 bell peppers
- Salt to taste
- 4 slices of sandwich bread
- Pepper to taste
- Extra virgin olive oil
- Finely chopped parsley

Instructions:
Wash and thoroughly dry the bell peppers.
Place them in the basket and cook at 390°F (200°C) for 20 minutes. Halfway through the cooking time, turn them over. Once they have cooled down a bit, peel them and cut them into thin strips. Season them with extra virgin olive oil, salt, pepper, and finely chopped parsley.
Toast the bread slices for six minutes at 370°F (190°C), turning them over to brown both sides. Top with the peppers and serve.
Smart Tip: As soon as the peppers are done cooking, seal them in a freezer bag while they are still hot and let them cool down. This will make peeling easier and faster.

BREADED VEGETABLE STICKS

Servings: 4 people
Difficulty: Easy
Cooking Time: 11 minutes

Ingredients:
- 2 zucchinis
- 1 bell pepper
- 2 carrots
- 2 eggs
- 6 slices of sandwich bread
- All-purpose flour (as needed)
- Olive oil (as needed)
- Salt (as needed)

Instructions:
Clean all the vegetables, wash them, and cut them into sticks about 0.4 inches thick.
Bring a large pot of salted water to a boil. First, blanch the carrots. After two minutes, add the bell pepper, and after another two minutes, add the zucchini. Cook everything for an additional minute, and then drain the vegetables on a kitchen towel.
In a mixer, grind the sandwich bread slices.
Dredge the vegetable sticks in flour, dip them in the beaten eggs seasoned with a pinch of salt, and then coat them with the ground bread, pressing firmly to ensure the bread adheres to the surface.
Line them up on the air fryer tray covered with a perforated parchment paper sheet, drizzle them with olive oil, and cook at 390°F for 11 minutes, turning them halfway through. Serve hot.
Tip: For crisper breading, after coating them with the ground bread, dip them again in the egg and then in the breadcrumbs.

FLAVORED MIXED VEGETABLES

Servings: 4 people
Difficulty: Easy
Cooking Time: 12 minutes

Ingredients:
- 2 zucchinis
- 2 eggplants
- 3 bell peppers (yellow, green, and red)
- 1 tsp. of olive oil
- Herbs of choice to taste
- 1 onion
- Salt to taste

Instructions:
Wash all the vegetables under running water and dry them with a clean cloth.
Trim the zucchinis and eggplants at the ends and dice them into small pieces.
Clean the bell peppers by removing the stem and seeds, then slice them into strips and then into pieces.
Clean the onion and slice it thinly.
In a bowl, combine all the vegetables and season with salt, olive oil, and chopped herbs (basil, mint, oregano, parsley, and garlic).
Mix well to evenly coat the vegetables and let them marinate for about an hour, covered with plastic wrap.
Place them in the air fryer and cook for about 12 minutes at 390°F, stirring occasionally.

GRILLED EGGPLANTS

Servings: 2 people
Difficulty: Easy
Cooking Time: 10 minutes

Ingredients:
- 2 eggplants
- Canned tuna
- Grana cheese flakes to taste
- Half a bunch of arugula
- Olive oil to taste
- Salt to taste
- Pepper to taste
- Apple cider vinegar to taste

Instructions:
Wash and trim the eggplants, then slice them about ⅓ inch thick widthwise.
Place them on the air fryer grill and cook at 370°F for ten minutes, turning halfway through.
In a bowl, combine salt, pepper, and apple cider vinegar. Mix until the salt dissolves, then add olive oil and mix again. Once the eggplants are cooked, dip them in the mixture and place them on a serving plate. Repeat with the remaining eggplants.
Spread the washed and dried arugula over the eggplants, add the drained tuna, and grate the Grana cheese over the top. Drizzle with more olive oil.
Note: Cooking times are approximate and depend on the thickness of the vegetables. The thinner they are, the shorter the cooking time

GRILLED ZUCCHINIS

Servings: 4 people
Difficulty: Easy
Cooking Time: 8 minutes

Ingredients:
- 3 zucchinis
- Olive oil to taste
- Paprika (sweet or spicy)
- Pepper to taste
- Salt to taste

Instructions:
Wash, dry, and trim the zucchinis. Slice them into rounds and place them in a large bowl.
Drizzle with olive oil and add the spices. Mix everything together, cover with plastic wrap, and let marinate for at least 30 minutes. After marinating, place the zucchini in the air fryer and set it to 370°F for eight minutes. Shake the basket to move the zucchinis around and continue cooking for another seven minutes.
Serve them warm, drizzling with more olive oil and adjusting the salt if needed. They are recommended as a side dish for fish dishes.

MOZZARELLA IN CARROZZA

Servings: 3 people
Difficulty: Medium-Easy
Cooking Time: 10 minutes

Ingredients:
- 6 slices of sandwich bread
- A few Tbsp.s of basil pesto 1 mozzarella
- Flour to taste
- 3 slices of mortadella
- 1 egg
- Crushed pistachios
- Bread crumbs to taste

Instructions:
Arrange 3 slices of bread on a plate; spread a tsp. of pesto on each.
Layer with a slice of mortadella, crushed pistachios, and a slice of mozzarella, and top with the remaining bread slices. Coat each sandwich in flour on all sides, then dip in the beaten egg with a pinch of salt, and finally, coat in bread crumbs, ensuring all sides are well-sealed. Repeat the coating process once more. Allow them to rest for a few minutes.
Place the sandwiches on the air fryer grill on perforated parchment paper. Cook at 370°F for ten minutes, turning halfway through.
Tip: You can also fill them with mozzarella and speck or mozzarella and two anchovy fillets

"FRIED" RICOTTA

Servings: 3 people
Difficulty: Medium-Easy
Cooking Time: 10 minutes

Ingredients:
- 1 ricotta cheese
- Flour to taste
- Salt to taste
- 2 eggs
- Pepper to taste
- Bread crumbs to taste

Instructions:
Slice the ricotta cheese about ⅕ inch thick and let it drain for five to six hours, preferably overnight (it should be dry to remain compact during cooking).
Prepare three plates: one with flour, one with beaten eggs, and one with bread crumbs.
Take the ricotta slices, season with salt and pepper, and coat them in flour, then egg, and finally bread crumbs. Repeat the coating process for a thicker crust.
Place them on the air fryer grill on perforated parchment paper.
Cook at 390°F for ten minutes, gently turning them after five minutes for even browning.

ONION AND OLIVE SPIRALS

Servings: 6 people
Difficulty: Medium-High
Cooking Time: 10 minutes

Ingredients:
- 4 1\3 cups of all-purpose flour
- 1 1\3 cups of water
- 3 Tbsp. of olive oil
- 1 tsp. of sugar
- 0.4 oz. of active dry yeast
- Salt to taste

Filling:
- 4-5 onions
- Pitted black olives
- Olive oil
- Salt
- 3-4 Tbsp. of grated cheese

Instructions:
In a bowl or mixer, combine all the ingredients and knead. Add salt and continue kneading until you get a soft but not sticky dough.
Let it rise until doubled in size, covered with an inverted bowl or plastic wrap (about two hours).
Meanwhile, peel and thinly slice the onions. Sauté them in a pan with some olive oil until wilted. Season with salt, add cheese and olives, and let it cool.
Roll out the dough into a rectangle, spread the onion mixture, leaving 1\4 inch from the top edge. Brush the edge with water, and roll it up.
Slice into 1\4 inch thick pieces and place them on perforated parchment paper. Let them rise for another hour.
Transfer the spirals with the parchment paper to the air fryer grill and set the temperature to 350°F, cooking for ten minutes.
Tip: Instead of grated cheese, you can add smoked scamorza or provolone cheese in small pieces.

ZUCCHINI FRITTATA

Servings: 6 people
Difficulty: Easy
Cooking Time: 30 minutes

Ingredients:
- 2 zucchinis
- 3 eggs
- 1 stale bread roll
- 3-4 Tbsp of grated cheese
- Greek feta cheese
- Salt
- Pepper
- Water or milk

Instructions:
Quarter the bread roll and soak it in water or milk.
Wash, dry, and dice the zucchini.
In a bowl, combine zucchini, grated cheese, soaked and squeezed bread, eggs, salt, and pepper. Mix until somewhat soft, then add cubed feta cheese.
Grease a 8 in-diameter baking dish, pour in the mixture, and flatten with a fork. Bake at 380°F for 25-30 minutes.

ZUCCHINI ROLLS WITH HAM AND MOZZARELLA

Servings: 4 people
Difficulty: Easy
Cooking Time: 6 minutes

Ingredients:
- 1-2 zucchinis, depending on size
- Bread crumbs to taste 3.5 oz sliced cooked ham
- Salt to taste
- 1 pack of small mozzarella balls
- Pepper to taste

Instructions:
Wash and trim the zucchini, then thinly slice them. Spray with oil and grill in the air fryer at 380°F for six minutes.
Cut the ham slices to fit the zucchini slices.
Once the zucchinis are cooked, lay them out and season both sides with salt and pepper.
Top each zucchini slice with a slice of ham and a mozzarella ball.
Roll them up, coat them in bread crumbs, and secure them with a toothpick.

ZUCCHINI FLOWERS WITH SMOKED CHEESE AND HAM

Servings: 4 people
Difficulty: Medium-Easy
Cooking Time: 18 minutes

Ingredients:
- 12 zucchini flowers
- 2 eggs
- ½ smoked provolone cheese
- Bread crumbs to taste
- 3 slices cooked ham
- Salt Flour to taste
- Pepper

Instructions:
Clean and wash the zucchini flowers. Season them with salt and pepper.
Cut the smoked provolone cheese into sticks about 0.4 inches wide and 0.8 inches long.
Cut each ham slice into four strips, wrap them around a cheese stick, and insert the combination into a zucchini flower.
Beat the eggs and add a pinch of salt.
Coat the zucchini flowers in flour, then dip them in the beaten eggs, and finally, coat them in bread crumbs, ensuring the tops are sealed.
Place the prepared zucchini flowers on the grill and preheat the air fryer to 390°F for three minutes. Cook at 380°F for about 15 minutes, gently turning them halfway through the cooking time.

ZUCCHINI FLOWERS WITH RICOTTA AND MINT

Servings: 4 people
Difficulty: Medium-Easy
Cooking Time: 15 minutes

Ingredients:
- 12 zucchini flowers
- Flour to taste
- 1 ricotta cheese
- 2 eggs
- 1-2 sprigs of mint
- Grated zest of ½ lemon
- Bread crumbs to taste
- Salt

Instructions:
Clean and wash the zucchini flowers.
In a bowl, beat the ricotta with salt and pepper. Add finely chopped mint leaves and lemon zest. Mix well and use the mixture to fill the zucchini flowers.
Beat the eggs with a pinch of salt.
Coat the zucchini flowers in flour, then dip them in the beaten eggs, and finally, coat them in bread crumbs, ensuring the tops are sealed.
Place the prepared zucchini flowers on the grill and preheat the air fryer to 390°F for three minutes.
Cook at 380°F for about 15 minutes, gently turning them halfway through the cooking time.

EGGPLANT "BRUSCHETTA"

Servings: 4 people
Difficulty: Easy
Cooking Time: 15 minutes

Ingredients:
- 2 eggplants
- 2 Tbsp. capers
- Oregano
- 1 cup of cherry
- Salt
- tomatoes
- 1 mozzarella cheese

Instructions:
Wash, trim, and slice the eggplants into 1\4 inch thick slices. Season them in a bowl with some salt and a little oil.
Place the seasoned eggplant slices on your air fryer grill and cook at 390°F for 15 minutes.
Meanwhile, wash and chop the cherry tomatoes. Add cubed mozzarella, capers, and anchovies. Season with salt, oregano, and oil. Let it rest for a few minutes.
Arrange the cooked eggplant slices side by side on a serving plate. Top with the tomato and mozzarella mixture, and serve.
Tip: You can put them back on the grill at 370°F for five to six minutes to melt the mozzarella and lightly cook the tomatoes

EGGPLANT CUTLET

Servings: 4 people
Difficulty: Medium
Cooking Time: 15 minutes

Ingredients:
- 2 eggplants
- 1.7 oz grated cheese Garlic powder
- Salt
- 1\2 cup of bread crumbs
- Pepper

Instructions:
Wash, dry, and trim the eggplants. Slice them about 1\4 inch thick.
In a bowl, combine the bread crumbs, grated cheese, garlic powder, salt, and pepper.
Beat the eggs with a pinch of salt, dip the eggplant slices in the egg, then in the bread crumbs, and place them on the air fryer grill. Cook at 390°F for 15 minutes.

BREADED BREAD

Servings: 2 people
Difficulty: Easy
Cooking Time: 6 minutes

Ingredients:
- 4 slices of stale bread, about 0.4 in. thick
- Bread crumbs
- 1 egg
- 1\4 cup of milk
- 2 Tbsp. of grated cheese
- Salt

Instructions:
Beat the eggs with a pinch of salt, add the cheese and milk, and continue mixing.
Dip the bread slices in the mixture, then in the bread crumbs.
Place the breaded slices on the air fryer grill and cook at 390°F for three minutes. Turn them over and cook for another three minutes.

ROSEMARY BREAD CUBES

Servings: 2 people
Difficulty: Easy
Cooking Time: 4 minutes

Ingredients:
- 5.3 oz baguettes or homemade bread
- 2 sprigs of rosemary
- Olive oil
- Garlic powder
- Oregano
- Salt

Instructions:
Cut the bread into cubes and place in a bowl.
Drizzle with olive oil and season with a couple of pinches of oregano, rosemary, garlic powder, and a pinch of salt.
Mix everything and place on the air fryer grill set at 390°F for four minutes, shaking occasionally to brown evenly.
Tip: These croutons can be served with chickpea soup or pumpkin velouté

CHILI PEPPER BREAD CUBES

Servings: 2 people
Difficulty: Easy
Cooking Time: 4 minutes

Ingredients:
- 2\3 cup of sliced bread
- Garlic powder
- Olive oil
- Salt Chili powder

Instructions:
Cut the bread into cubes and place them in a bowl.
Drizzle with olive oil and season with garlic powder, a pinch of salt, and ground chili pepper.
Mix everything and place on the air fryer grill set at 390°F for four minutes, shaking occasionally to brown evenly.
Tip: These croutons can be served with minestrone or legume soups.

MUFFINS WITH ZUCCHINI AND SUN-DRIED TOMATOES

Servings: 8 muffins
Difficulty: Medium-Easy
Cooking Time: 15 minutes

Ingredients:
- 2 eggs
- 2\3 cup of all-purpose flour
- 5 sun-dried tomatoes in oil
- 1.7 oz grated Parmesan cheese
- ½ packet of baking powder for savory cakes
- 1 zucchini
- 1\3 cup of milk
- Salt to taste
- 1\8 cup of vegetable oil
- Black sesame seeds

Instructions:
Wash, dry, and trim the zucchini. Grate it finely, season with a couple of pinches of salt, and let it marinate.
In the meantime, in a bowl, combine the flour, baking powder, and cheese. Add the eggs, milk, and oil, mixing until you get a dense, smooth batter. Cut the sun-dried tomatoes into small pieces, drained of their oil, and add them to the batter.
Finally, add the zucchini, having squeezed out any excess water, and mix everything together.
Cut squares from parchment paper, wet them, wring them out, and use them to line individual round aluminum molds that will fit in your air fryer. Fill the molds with the mixture, leaving 1\4 inch from the edge.
Sprinkle with sesame seeds and bake at 370°F for 15 minutes. Check with a toothpick to ensure it is cooked through.

TOMINI WRAPPED IN BACON

Servings: 4 people
Difficulty: Easy
Cooking Time: 6 minutes

Ingredients:
- 4 mini cheese
- 8 slices of bacon

Instructions:
On a sheet of parchment paper, place two slices of bacon crossed over each other and place a tomato cheese on top. Make an incision and wrap the cheese completely with the bacon slices.
Cook at 320°F for six minutes.

TOMINI WITH WALNUTS AND DRIED FIGS

Servings: 4 people
Difficulty: Easy
Cooking Time: 10 minutes

Ingredients:
- 4 mini cheese
- 1 sprig of rosemary
- 8 walnut kernels
- 2 tsp. of honey
- 5 dried figs

Instructions:
Grind the walnuts, figs, and rosemary in a mixer.
On a sheet of parchment paper, place the mini cheese and make an incision. Sprinkle them with the dried fruit mixture and a bit of honey, and cook at 360°F for ten minutes.
Tip: Dried figs can be replaced with dates, prunes, or other dried fruit of your choice.

ARTICHOKE FLANS WITH GORGONZOLA SAUCE

Servings: 4 people
Difficulty: Medium-High
Cooking Time: 34 minutes

Ingredients:
- 3 artichokes
- 3 eggs
- 4.2 oz grated cheese
- 1\3 cup of bread crumbs
- 1 garlic clove
- 2\3 cup of béchamel sauce
- Salt to taste

For the Gorgonzola Sauce:
- 2.8 oz gorgonzola cheese
- 1\4 cup of cream or milk
- 1 lemon
- Olive oil
- White wine to taste Butter to taste

Instructions:
Fill a bowl with water and squeeze in the lemon.
Clean the artichokes, slice them, and place them in the bowl with water and lemon.
In a pan, add some oil, the crushed, unpeeled garlic clove, and the drained artichokes. Brown everything in your air fryer set at 370°F for about eight minutes, stirring halfway through. Add some wine and continue cooking for another five minutes, seasoning with salt. Let it cool. Once cooled, remove the garlic clove and chop the artichokes with a knife. In a bowl, combine the artichokes with the béchamel, eggs, grated cheese, and bread crumbs. Mix everything together.
Cut squares from parchment paper, wet them, wring them out, and use them to line individual molds. Fill the molds with the mixture. Cook at 370°F for 21 minutes.
Meanwhile, in a saucepan, melt the gorgonzola with the cream and serve it on the flans.
Tip: You can also use other vegetables according to your tastes. Great with zucchini or asparagus.

SPINACH MEDALLIONS

Servings: 2 people (8 medallions)
Difficulty: Easy
Cooking Time: 13 minutes

Ingredients:
- 1 1\3 cups of frozen
- 2\3 cup of bread crumbs
- spinach 1 egg
- Salt to taste
- 2.8 oz grated cheese

Instructions:
Place the spinach in a baking dish and cook at 340°F for 13 minutes.
Once cooked, finely chop the spinach with a knife and place in a bowl along with bread crumbs, cheese, egg, and salt. Form small balls the size of a small plum and flatten them.
Coat them in bread crumbs and place them on squares of parchment paper on the air fryer grill. Cook at 360°F for 13 minutes, turning halfway through.

PUFF PASTRY RUSTIC WITH STEWED TURNIP TOPS

Servings: 4 people
Difficulty: Medium-High
Cooking Time: 13 minutes (plus turnip

Ingredients:
- Olive oil to taste
- 2 rolls of puff pastry
- Salt to taste
- 1 2\3 cups of turnip tops
- 3 bay leaves
- tops cooking time)
- 2 garlic cloves
- 1 chili pepper (optional)

Instructions:
Clean the turnip tops by picking the florets. If they are large, split them in half, wash them, and blanch them in salted water for five minutes. In a pan with oil, sauté the crushed, unpeeled garlic and chopped chili pepper. Tilt the pan to one side to flavor the oil without burning it. Add the bay leaves. Drain the turnip tops and add them to the pan with the flavored oil, season with salt and add half a glass of the cooking water. Cook on low heat for about 20 minutes, stirring occasionally. They should be dry and easily crumble when pressed with a fork. Remove the garlic and bay leaves and let it cool.
Roll out the puff pastry and cut out 3 inches diameter discs. Fill them with the mixture in the center, making sure to leave the edges free. Brush with water and seal the edges. Cut squares from parchment paper the size of your rustic pastries and place them on the air fryer grill. Cook at 370°F for 13 minutes.

FRIGGITELLI WITH COARSE SALT

Servings: 2 people
Difficulty: Easy
Cooking Time: 14 minutes

Ingredients:
- 1 1\3 cups of friggitelli (small greenpeppers)
- Coarse salt to taste
- Olive oil to taste

Instructions:
Wash and dry the friggitelli.
Place them on the air fryer grill, drizzle with olive oil, and sprinkle with coarse salt.
Cook at 370°F for 14 minutes, turning them occasionally.

CROSTINI WITH FRIGGITELLI AND CHERRY TOMATOES

Servings: 2 people
Difficulty: Easy
Cooking Time: 19 minutes

Ingredients:
- 1 1\3 cups of friggitelli
- 5 red battering tomatoes
- Olive oil to taste
- Salt to taste 5 yellow battering tomatoes
- 1 baguette

Instructions:
Wash and dry the friggitelli. Place them on the air fryer grill, drizzle with olive oil, and cook at 370°F for 14 minutes, turning them occasionally.
Meanwhile, wash and quarter the cherry tomatoes, place them in a container, season with salt and oil, and let them marinate. Slice the baguette, drizzle with olive oil, and toast at 370°F for five minutes, turning halfway through.
Combine the friggitelli with the cherry tomatoes and serve on the crostini.

SPRING ROLLS

Servings: 2 people
Difficulty: Medium-Easy
Cooking Time: 10 minutes

Ingredients:
- 1 roll of phyllo dough
- 1 onion
- 1 zucchini
- 1 1\2 tbsp. soy sauce
- 2 carrots

Instructions:
Slice the zucchini, onion, and carrots into very thin strips.
In a pan with oil, sauté the vegetables for about five minutes, adding the soy sauce halfway through the cooking time. Roll out the phyllo dough and cut into four rectangles.
Place the vegetable filling in the center and fold securely.
Brush the rolls with a Tbsp. of oil and cook on the air fryer grill at 390°F for ten minutes.

PUFF PASTRY GRISSINI WITH SPECK AND CHEESE

Servings: 2 people
Difficulty: Easy
Cooking Time: 13 minutes

Ingredients:
- 1 rectangular roll of puff pastry
- 1 egg yolk
- 1.7 oz grated cheese of your choice
- Poppy seeds to taste
- 8 slices of speck, salami, or coppa

Instructions:
Unroll the puff pastry and place the speck slices on half of the pastry. Sprinkle with grated cheese and cover with the other half of the pastry, folding it over.
Brush with beaten egg yolk and sprinkle with poppy seeds.
Cut the pastry into 1\4 inch wide strips using a pastry wheel. Twist the ends of each strip. Place them on the air fryer grill with perforated parchment paper and cook at 360°F for 13 minutes.
Halfway through the cooking time, shake them to ensure even cooking.
Serve your grissini directly in a jar or glass, or simply tie it with a ribbon and serve it on a cutting board.

WURSTEL RUSTIC

Servings: 4 people
Difficulty: Easy
Cooking Time: 13 minutes

Ingredients:
- 1 rectangular roll of puff pastry
- 8 small wurstels (sausages)

Instructions:
Unroll the puff pastry and cut a strip the length of the wurst.
Wrap the wurstel inside, overlapping just enough to close. Seal the ends well to prevent the pastry from opening during cooking.
Cut each wurstel into five pieces and place them on the air fryer grill with perforated parchment paper. Cook at 370°F for 13 minutes, shaking halfway through.

SPINACH CROQUETTES WITH MELTING HEART

Servings: 2 people (8 croquettes)
Difficulty: Easy
Cooking Time: 13 minutes

Ingredients:
- 1 1\3 cups of frozen spinach
- 2\3 cup of bread crumbs
- 2.8 oz grated cheese
- 1 egg
- Cheese (Cheddar, Emmental, Galbanino, Scamorza)
- Salt to taste

Instructions:
Place the spinach in a baking dish and cook at 340°F for 13 minutes. Once cooked, chop finely with a knife and place it in a bowl with bread crumbs, grated cheese, egg, and salt.
Cut the cheese into eight strips, about 0.4 inches wide and 1.2 inches long.
Form balls using the spinach mixture, flatten them, place the cheese in the center, and seal well, ensuring the edges are sealed to prevent the cheese from leaking during cooking.
Dip them in egg and bread crumbs and place them on squares of parchment paper on the air fryer grill. Cook at 360°F for 13 minutes, shaking halfway through.

TOMATO AND MOZZARELLA RUSTIC

Servings: 4 people (8 rustic)
Difficulty: Medium-Easy
Cooking Time: 13 minutes

Ingredients:
- 2 rectangular rolls of puff pastry
- Tomato paste
- 3.5 oz mozzarella
- 1 egg yolk 1 Tbsp. milk

For the Bechamel:
- 1\4 cup of flour
- 1 oz butter
- 1 cup of milk

Instructions:
Unroll the puff pastry and cut out 16 discs using a glass or cookie cutter.
In a saucepan, melt the butter, add the flour, and stir until lightly browned. Add the milk all at once and cook for five minutes (until thickened). Remove from heat, add the chopped mozzarella, and stir until melted. Let it cool with plastic wrap directly touching the bechamel to prevent skin from forming.
Place a Tbsp. of tomato paste and a generous Tbsp. of bechamel in the center of eight discs. Wet the edges with a brush and cover with another disc of puff pastry, pressing well to seal. Brush with a mixture of egg yolk and milk.
Place them on squares of parchment paper and cook in the air fryer at 370°F for 13 minutes.

PUFF PASTRY CONES WITH CHEESE CREAM

Servings: 4 people (12 cones)
Difficulty: Medium-Easy
Cooking Time: 13 minutes

Ingredients:
- 1 rectangular puff pastry
- 2 heaped Tbsp. of grated Emmental
- 1 egg
- 2 heaped Tbsp. of grated parmesan
- 1\4 cup of butter
- Nutmeg to taste
- 1\8 cup of flour
- Salt to taste
- 2 cups of milk
- Freshly ground pepper to taste

Instructions:
Unroll the puff pastry and cut 0.6 in. wide strips. Wrap the strips around cone molds, slightly overlapping, and place them on the air fryer grill with perforated parchment paper. Brush with egg white. Cook at 360°F for 13 minutes.
If you don't have cone molds, you can make them using aluminum foil.
In a saucepan, melt the butter, add the flour, and stir until lightly browned. Add the milk all at once and cook for five minutes, stirring continuously. Remove from heat, and season with salt, pepper, and grated nutmeg.
Add the egg yolk and grated cheese, stirring vigorously until melted. Let it cool, and cover it with plastic wrap touching the surface.
Once cooled, stir well to soften, pour it into a pastry bag, and fill the cones.

LEMON-SCENTED EGG SALAD

Servings: 2 people
Difficulty: Easy
Cooking Time: 15 minutes

Ingredients:
- 4 eggs
- 4 tsp. of olive oil
- 3 sprigs of parsley
- Salt
- 1 lemon
- Freshly ground pepper

Instructions:
Hard boil the eggs in the air fryer at 270°F for 15 minutes. Cool in a bowl with very cold water.
Peel the eggs and chop them.
Chop the parsley and squeeze the lemon.
Place the eggs on a serving plate, add the chopped parsley, lemon juice, and a drizzle of olive oil, and serve.

GREEN BEAN SALAD WITH SOFT-BOILED EGGS

Servings: 2 people
Difficulty: Easy
Cooking Time: 12 minutes

Ingredients:
- 4 eggs
- Olive oil
- Salt
- Green beans
- Pepper

Instructions:
Wash and trim the green beans. Boil them in water until tender.
Drain and season with salt and olive oil.
Meanwhile, place the eggs in the air fryer basket and set the machine to 270°F for 12 minutes.
Cool the eggs in cold or ice water, peel them, and place them on the bed of green beans.
Season everything with a pinch of salt, a grind of pepper, and another drizzle of olive oil.

ONION AND GORGONZOLA QUICHE

Servings: 2 people
Difficulty: Easy
Cooking Time: 20 minutes

Ingredients:
- 3\4 cup of flour
- 1.8 oz Parmesan cheese
- 1\3 cup of room temperature butter
- 2 onions Salt to taste
- 3.5 oz Gorgonzola cheese
- 1\3 cups of cold water
- Olive oil
- 2 eggs
- Salt to taste

Instructions:
In a bowl, combine the flour, water, butter and salt, and knead until you get a homogeneous dough. Wrap it in plastic wrap and let it rest for about an hour.
Peel and finely slice the onions. Cook them in a pan with a little oil for five minutes, covered, and let them cool.
After resting, work the dough a bit to slightly warm it and roll it out on parchment paper, slightly larger than the diameter of your pan. Flip the rolled-out disc onto the pan and raise the edges.
Add the onion and pieces of Gorgonzola.
Break the eggs into a bowl, beat them with a pinch of salt and grated cheese, and pour it over the onion.
Adjust the edges by turning them inwards for a bit of movement. Bake in your air fryer at 370°F for about 20 minutes. The edges should be golden, and the egg set.

HAM AND MOZZARELLA QUICHE

Servings: 2 people
Difficulty: Easy
Cooking Time: 20 minutes

Ingredients:
- 3\4 cup of flour
- 1.8 oz Parmesan cheese
- 1\2 cup of room temperature butter
- 3 slices of cooked ham
- 5.3 oz Mozzarella
- 1\3 cup of cold water
- 3.5 oz Fontina cheese
- 2 eggs
- Salt to taste

Instructions:
In a bowl, combine the flour, butter, salt and water, and knead until you get a homogeneous dough. Wrap it in plastic wrap and let it rest for about an hour.
After resting, work the dough a bit to slightly warm it and roll it out on parchment paper, slightly larger than the diameter of your pan. Flip the rolled-out disc onto the pan and raise the edges.
Add the slices of cooked ham, Fontina, and slightly overlapping slices of Mozzarella.
Break the eggs into a bowl, beat them with a pinch of salt and grated Parmesan cheese, and pour it over the quiche.
Adjust the edges by turning them inwards for a bit of movement. Bake at 370°F for about 20 minutes in the air fryer. The edges should be golden, and the egg set.

ZUCCHINI AND ROBIOLA ROLLS

Servings: 2 people
Difficulty: Easy
Cooking Time: 6 minutes

Ingredients:
- 14 slices of zucchini
- 1.8 oz raw ham
- 4.2 oz Robiola cheese
- A small bunch of chives
- Salt to taste
- Pepper to taste

Instructions:
Wash and dry the zucchini. Obtain 14 slices of the same size.
Spray them with a little oil on both sides and grill them, setting the air fryer to 380°F for six minutes.
In a bowl, combine the Robiola, chives, and chopped raw ham, and mix everything into a cream. Let it rest in the fridge for about 30 minutes.
When the zucchini slices have cooled, spread the Robiola cream with a knife, roll up the zucchini, and close with a strand of chive.

PUMPKIN CHIPS

Servings: 2 people
Difficulty: Easy
Cooking Time: 8-10 minutes

Ingredients:
- 1 1\3 cups of cleaned pumpkin
- Olive oil to taste
- Salt to taste Pepper to taste

Instructions:
Slice the pumpkin with a mandolin to a thickness of 1\4 inch and place it on a clean and dry cloth. Pat the slices well to dry them. Place them in a bowl, spray them with a little oil, and add a bit of pepper. Mix and place the right amount of product on the grill without piling up too much.
Set your air fryer to 370°F for eight to ten minutes and shake during cooking. Once cooked, add a pinch of salt.

ROASTED PUMPKIN

Servings: 2 people
Difficulty: Easy
Cooking Time: 15 minutes

Ingredients:
- 1 1\3 cups of pumpkin
- Pepper to taste Olive oil to taste
- 2 sprigs of thyme

Instructions:
Wash and dry the pumpkin. Slice it and remove seeds and filaments.
Spray the slices with a little oil and place them on the grill, cooking at 360°F for 15 minutes, turning halfway.
At the end, pierce with a fork to check the cooking, as the timing can vary based on the thickness and quality of the pumpkin and the machine. Season with a drizzle of oil, thyme leaves, salt, and pepper.

"FRIED" ZUCCHINI FLOWERS IN BATTER

Servings: 2 people
Difficulty: Easy
Cooking Time: 15 minutes

Ingredients:
- 6 zucchini flowers
- 1 egg
- 6 anchovies
- 1.8 oz scamorza cheese
- 1\3 cup of flour
- Pepper to taste
- Cold water to taste
- Olive oil to taste
- Salt to taste

Instructions:
Wash and dry the zucchini flowers, removing the pistil.
In a bowl, break the egg and beat it with a pinch of salt; add the flour, and while mixing, add the very cold water. The batter should be smooth and lump-free.
Fill the zucchini flowers with a strip of scamorza and a slice of anchovy, close by slightly turning the top part, and dip them in the batter, placing them on parchment paper. Freeze.
Once well frozen, place them on perforated parchment paper, spray them with oil, and cook at 360°F for eight minutes. Turn them, spray a little more oil, and start again, raising to 380°F for another seven minutes.

BREAD MEATBALLS

Servings: 4 people
Difficulty: Easy
Cooking Time: 15 minutes

Ingredients:
- 3 stale rolls
- 1 garlic clove
- A small bunch of parsley
- 2 eggs
- 2.8 oz grated cheese
- Pepper to taste
- Salt to taste
- Olive oil to taste

Instructions:
Soak the bread in a bowl with water. Squeeze it well and place it in another bowl with the eggs, cheese, finely chopped parsley, garlic, salt, and pepper. Mix everything and form balls.
Spray them with oil and cook at 380°F for 15 minutes, shaking several times during cooking to brown on all sides.

EGGPLANT MEATBALLS

Servings: 4 people
Difficulty: Easy
Cooking Time: 27 minutes

Ingredients:
- 3 stale rolls
- 1 eggplant
- 1 garlic clove
- 2 eggs
- 2.8 oz grated cheese
- 2 small bunches of mint
- Olive oil to taste
- Salt to taste
- Pepper to taste

Instructions:
Soak the bread in a bowl with water.
Dice the eggplant, spray it with a bit of oil, and cook at 360°F for seven minutes. Let it cool.
Squeeze the bread well and place it in another bowl with the eggs, eggplant, cheese, finely chopped mint, garlic, salt, and pepper. Mix everything and form balls.
Spray them with oil and cook at 390°F for 20 minutes, shaking several times during cooking to brown on all sides.

SALMON AND AVOCADO BAGELS

Servings: 4 people
Difficulty: High
Cooking Time: 30 minutes

Ingredients:
- 1 1\2 cups of flour
- 3\4 cups of water
- 1\3 tbsp brewer's yeast
- 1\2 tbsp honey
- Salt to taste

For the filling:
- 5.3 oz smoked salmon
- 0.35 oz goat cheese
- 1\2 cup of grilled zucchini
- ½ avocado
- 1 lime

Instructions:
In a small bowl, dissolve the brewer's yeast in a bit of lukewarm water and honey. In another bowl, add the flour, remaining water, and yeast mixture. Knead by hand until you get a smooth dough. Add salt and knead again until fully absorbed.
Place the dough in a bowl, cover it with plastic wrap, and let it rise until it triples in volume (about three to four hours). Divide the dough into six pieces and form rings with a diameter of about 3 inches. Place them on squares of parchment paper and let them rise until doubled in size (about another hour), covered with a cloth.
Bring water to a boil in a pot. Take the bagels with their paper and boil them for about a minute, turning halfway. Drain them with a slotted spoon and place them on perforated parchment paper. Cook in your air fryer at 370°F for 30 minutes.
Once cooled, cut them in half and spread each half with goat cheese; add grilled zucchini, salmon, avocado slices, a bit of lime juice, and freshly ground pepper.

BRESAOLA, ARUGULA, AND GRANA BAGELS

Servings: 4 people
Difficulty: High
Cooking Time: 30 minutes

Ingredients:
- 1 1\2 cups of flour
- 3\4 cups of water
- 1\3 tbsp brewer's yeast
- 1\2 tbsp honey
- Salt to taste

For the filling :
- 5.3 oz bresaola
- 0.35 oz goat cheese
- A bunch of arugula
- 1.8 oz Grana cheese shavings
- ½ lemon
- Olive oil
- Pepper to taste

Instructions:
Follow the same procedure for the bagel dough as the Salmon and Avocado Bagels.
Once cooled, cut them in half and spread each half with goat cheese, add torn arugula leaves and slices of bresaola, and drizzle with extra virgin olive oil, a few drops of lemon juice, some black pepper, and Grana cheese shavings.

SURPRISE TOMATOES

Servings: 4 people
Difficulty: Easy
Cooking Time: 20 minutes

Ingredients:
- 4 large red tomatoes
- 4 spring onions
- 4 eggs
- 2.1 oz grated cheese
- 2.1 oz mozzarella
- Salt to taste
- Pepper to taste

Instructions:
Wash and dry the tomatoes, leaving the stem. Cut the tops off ⅔ of their height and empty the tomatoes of their pulp using a spoon. Chop the spring onions and mozzarella and distribute them in the tomatoes.
Break an egg into each tomato, sprinkle with grated cheese, and a grind of pepper.
Place the filled tomatoes in a baking dish and put the tops back on. Cook in the air fryer at 370°F for 15-20 minutes.

BAKED TOMATO AND MOZZARELLA CALZONES

Servings: 4 calzones
Difficulty: Easy
Cooking Time: 8 minutes

Ingredients:
- 1 1\3 cups of flour
- 1\2 cups of water
- 1\3 tbsp brewer's yeast
- Salt to taste

For the filling:
- 3.5 oz mozzarella
- Tomato puree
- Oregano to taste
- 1 pinch of salt
- 1 tsp. olive oil

Instructions:
Chop the mozzarella and let it drain in a colander for a couple of hours. In a bowl, pour the flour.
Dissolve the brewer's yeast in water at room temperature (neither cold nor hot) with a pinch of sugar to activate the yeast.
Add the water with the dissolved yeast to the flour while mixing with your hands or with the mixer hook.
Add the olive oil and knead. Finally, add the salt and knead until it's well combined.
Form a dough ball, work it on the work surface, and place it in a bowl to rise in a turned-off oven, covered with plastic wrap, for about an hour (until doubled in size).
Take the dough, turn it out onto the work surface, and divide it into four small dough balls. Roll them out to form a disk three to four milimeters thick. Season the tomato puree with a pinch of salt, oregano, and a drop of oil.
On half of each disk, place a spoonful of tomato puree and some mozzarella. Fold into a half-moon shape, sealing the edges of the calzone with a fork. Brush the surface with olive oil and sprinkle with salt and oregano.
Place the calzones directly on the air fryer. Cook at 380°F for seven to ten minutes, turning them halfway for even cooking.

POTATO CROQUETTES

Servings: 4 people
Difficulty: Easy
Cooking Time: 6 minutes

Ingredients:
- 2 cups of potatoes
- 1 egg for breading
- 1 egg
- Bread crumbs to taste
- 3.5 oz grated cheese
- Flour to taste
- Salt to taste
- 1 pinch of nutmeg
- Pepper to taste

Instructions:
Wash the potatoes and place them in a pot. Cover with water at room temperature and bring to a boil. This will take about 40 minutes.
Let them cool slightly, peel them, and mash them in a bowl. Add salt and pepper, and grate some nutmeg. Add the cheese and, finally, the whole egg. Mix everything. You will get a dry and homogeneous mixture.
Prepare three plates: in the first, place some flour; in the second, the beaten egg; and in the third, the bread crumbs. Take some of the mixture and shape it into a small cylinder. First, coat it in flour, then in the egg, and finally in the bread crumbs. If you prefer a thicker breading, you can repeat the process twice.
Continue in the same way until all the mixture is used up.
Lightly oil the air fryer basket, place the croquettes, spray them with a bit of oil, and bake at 390°F for six minutes, turning often to achieve a nice golden color.

POTATO MILLEFEUILLE WITH SPECK AND SMOKED SCAMORZA

Servings: 4 people
Difficulty: Easy
Cooking Time: 30 minutes

Ingredients:
- 5 potatoes
- 3.5 oz smoked scamorza
- 3.5 oz grated parmesan cheese
- Bread crumbs
- 3.5 oz speck
- Extra virgin olive oil to taste

Instructions:
Peel the potatoes, rinse them well, and slice them with a mandolin. Season with salt, pepper, and a drizzle of extra virgin olive oil and mix.
In a baking dish, drizzle some oil, arrange the potato slices slightly overlapping to avoid empty spaces, create a layer of speck and smoked scamorza, sprinkle with grated cheese, and repeat the process, alternating more potatoes with speck and cheese, finishing with the last layer of potatoes.
Sprinkle with some bread crumbs and the remaining grated cheese. Bake in the air fryer at 360°F for 30 minutes.

LIME AND PINK PEPPER CHIPS (SAN CARLO STYLE)

Servings: 4 people
Difficulty: Easy
Cooking Time: 25 minutes

Ingredients:
- 2 1\2 cups of potatoes
- 1-2 limes
- Fine salt to taste
- 1 Tbsp. of pink pepper
- Extra virgin olive oil to taste

Instructions:
Wash and dry the potatoes. Using a mandolin, slice them (with the skin on) to a thickness of three milimeters and soak them in very cold water for 30 minutes.
Drain them well and place them in a bowl with the chopped pink pepper, salt, lime juice, and a drizzle of oil. Let them marinate for about an hour.
Preheat the air fryer to 390°F for three minutes; drain the potatoes from the lime juice, drizzle with a bit of oil, mix well, and place them in the basket to cook at 390°F for 25 minutes, shaking several times during cooking.

HAM AND CHEESE TOAST

Servings: 4 people
Difficulty: Medium-Easy
Cooking Time: 6 minutes

Ingredients:
- 16 slices of sandwich bread
- 8 slices of Gruyère or cheddar cheese
- 8 slices of cooked ham
- 8 Tbsp. of béchamel sauce

Instructions:
Take the sandwich bread slices and place them on a cutting board. Spread them with a Tbsp. of béchamel sauce. Cover half of the slices with cooked ham and cheese and close with the other slice of sandwich bread.
Secure the slices by inserting four toothpicks, one on each side, ensuring that they do not deform during cooking. Preheat the air fryer to 390°F for three minutes and bake the toast, lowering the temperature to 360°F for six minutes, turning halfway through cooking to brown both sides.

HAM, CHEESE, ZUCCHINI, AND PESTO TOAST

Servings: 4 people
Difficulty: Medium-Easy
Cooking Time: 6 minutes

Ingredients:
- 16 slices of sandwich bread
- 16 slices of grilled zucchini
- 8 slices of Gruyère cheese
- 8 slices of cooked ham
- Pesto to taste

Instructions:
Place the sandwich bread slices on a cutting board. On half of them, place a couple of slices of grilled zucchini, some pesto, a slice of cooked ham, and cheese. Cover with the other slice of sandwich bread.
Secure the corners with toothpicks and cook at 360°F for six minutes in a preheated air fryer, turning halfway through.

COLORFUL CEREAL BRUSCHETTA

Servings: 4 people
Difficulty: Easy
Cooking Time: 2 minutes

Ingredients:
- 1 small Tropea onion
- 8 slices of cereal bread
- Extra virgin olive oil
- 1\4 cup of cherry tomatoes
- 1\4 cup of yellow battering tomatoes
- Salt to taste
- Pecorino cheese shavings to taste

Instructions:
Wash, dry, and quarter the cherry tomatoes. Season them with salt, oil, basil, and finely diced Tropea onion. Let them marinate for about 30 minutes. Toast the bread in a preheated air fryer at 390°F for two minutes.
Place the toasted bread on a serving plate or a nice cutting board, and top each slice with a generous spoonful of tomatoes and onion. Finish with some pecorino cheese shavings.

BRUSCHETTA WITH GRILLED ZUCCHINI, AVOCADO, AND SESAME TUNA

Servings: 4 people
Difficulty: Easy
Cooking Time: 23 minutes

Ingredients:
- 8 slices of whole wheat bread
- 1 tsp. of balsamic vinegar
- 1 zucchini
- 7 oz tuna
- Sesame seeds
- ½ avocado
- Extra virgin olive oil
- Pepper to taste
- Salt to taste
- Lemon juice to taste

Instructions:
Wash, dry, and trim the zucchini. Slice it thinly, spray it with oil, and grill at 370°F for 13 minutes. Season with salt, pepper, a drizzle of oil, and balsamic vinegar. Coat the tuna in sesame seeds and cook on the air fryer grill at 360°F for eight minutes, turning halfway through. Let it cool slightly and slice. Clean and slice the avocado. Season the slices with lemon juice, salt, and pepper. Toast the bread slices at 390°F for two minutes.
Assemble the bruschetta by placing grilled zucchini slices, avocado slices, and seared tuna slices on the toasted bread. Drizzle with extra virgin olive oil.

BRUSCHETTA WITH EGGS AND AVOCADO

Servings: 4 people
Difficulty: Easy
Cooking Time: 7 minutes

Ingredients:
- 8 slices of whole wheat or rye bread
- 4 eggs
- ½ avocado
- Extra virgin olive oil
- Lemon juice to taste
- Pepper to taste
- Salt to taste

Instructions:
Clean the avocado and slice it. Season the slices with a few drops of lemon juice, salt, and a pinch of pepper.
Toast the rye bread slices at 390°F for two minutes.
In a bowl, break the eggs, season with salt and pepper, and scramble. Cook in a pan sprayed with a bit of oil at 360°F for five minutes.
Assemble the bruschetta by placing the scrambled eggs and avocado slices on the toasted bread. Drizzle with a bit of extra virgin olive oil and serve.

BRUSCHETTA WITH STRACCHINO CHEESE AND SAUSAGE

Servings: 4 people
Difficulty: Easy
Cooking Time: 7 minutes

Ingredients:
- 8 slices of white bread
- 7 oz stracchino cheese
- 7 oz sausage

Instructions:
Remove the sausage casing and crumble it in a bowl with a fork.
Add the stracchino cheese and mix well to combine.
Spread the mixture on the bread slices. Preheat the air fryer to 390°F.
Bake the bruschettas at 370°F until the stracchino cheese melts and the sausage is cooked, about seven to eight minutes.

BRUSCHETTA WITH ROBIOLA, FIGS AND PROSCIUTTO CRUDO

Servings: 4
Difficulty: Easy Cooking
Time: 7 minutes

Ingredients:
- 8 slices of cereal bread
- 7 oz Robiola cheese
- 5.3 oz raw ham (Prosciutto Crudo)
- 1 tsp. of honey
- 8 figs
- Some thyme leaves
- Salt

Instructions:
Bread Toasting: Toast the bread at 390°F for two minutes, spraying both sides with a bit of oil.
Preparing Figs: Make a cross-cut on the figs without cutting all the way through, dividing them into four to form a flower shape. Brush them with honey and grill in the air fryer at 360°F for three minutes.
Cheese Mixture: Mix the Robiola cheese with a pinch of salt and chopped thyme.
Assembling: Take the toasted bread slices and spread them with the Robiola cheese mixture. Gently place the raw ham on top, making it voluminous. Decorate with the grilled figs.

BRUSCHETTA WITH STRACCIATELLA, MORTADELLA, AND PISTACHIOS

Servings: 4 people
Difficulty: Easy
Cooking Time: 2 minutes

Ingredients:
- 8 slices of potato bread
- 8 slices of Mortadella
- 4.2 oz Stracciatella cheese
- 1\4 cup of chopped pistachios

Instructions:
Bread Toasting: Toast the potato bread slices at 390°F for two minutes. Place them on a serving plate. Assembling: Place the Mortadella slices on the bread. Cover with a generous forkful of Stracciatella. Decorate with the chopped pistachios.

ONION RINGS IN BATTER

Servings: 4 people
Difficulty: Easy
Cooking Time: 13 minutes

Ingredients:
- 1 1\3 cups of white onion
- 1\4 cup of cold sparkling water
- 2 tbsp white wine vinegar
- 1\3 cup of flour
- 1 egg
- Salt to taste
- Pepper to taste
- Oil to taste

Instructions:
Onion Preparation: Peel the onions and cut them into approximately 5mm thick slices. Separate the rings and place them in a bowl with the vinegar to marinate for about 30 minutes. Drain the onions in a colander.
Batter Preparation: In the meantime, prepare the batter by beating the egg in a bowl with a pinch of salt and pepper. Add the flour and, while mixing, add the cold sparkling water. You should get a thick and smooth mixture.
Coating and Freezing: Dip the onion rings in the batter. Place them on a baking tray lined with parchment paper. Freeze for about an hour.
Air Frying: Preheat your air fryer to 390°F for three minutes. Place the onion rings on perforated parchment paper and spray with a little oil. Bake at 370°F for 13 minutes, shaking the basket halfway through. They should be golden and crispy; if not, continue cooking for a few more minutes.

CRISPY BACON, SCRAMBLED EGGS, AND TOASTED BREAD

Servings: 4 people
Difficulty: Easy
Cooking Time: 7 minutes

Ingredients:
- 3.5 oz bacon
- 8 slices of sandwich bread
- 4 eggs
- 1 tsp. of oil
- Salt to taste

Instructions:
Bacon Cooking: Preheat the air fryer to 390°F for three minutes. Place the bacon slices on the grill and cook at 390°F for about eight minutes. Scrambled Eggs: In the meantime, beat the eggs in a bowl with a bit of salt. Pour the mixture into a slightly oiled pan.
Start the air fryer at 340°F for five minutes, stirring often to "scramble" the eggs.
Bread Toasting: Toast the bread slices at 390°F for two minutes. Serve everything together.

MC-STYLE FRIES

Servings: 4 people
Difficulty: Easy
Cooking Time: 28 minutes

Ingredients:
- 1 2\3 cups of frozen potatoes
- Cheddar sauce
- 3.5 oz bacon
- 1 tsp cooking oil

Instructions:
Fry Preparation: Pour the potatoes into the air fryer basket. Spray them with a little oil spray. Cook at 390°F for about 20 minutes (they should be golden and crispy).
Bacon Grilling: Grill the bacon on the air fryer grill at 390°F for about eight minutes. Cut it into thin strips. Assembling: Place the grilled bacon strips on the potatoes. Season everything with the cheddar sauce.

OMELETTE

Servings: 2 people
Difficulty: Easy
Cooking Time: 9 minutes

Ingredients:
- 4 eggs
- 1 Tbsp. grated cheese
- Extra virgin olive oil
- Salt to taste
- Chives to taste
- Pepper to taste

Instructions:
Egg Mixture Preparation: Break the eggs into a bowl. Add a bit of salt and a pinch of pepper, and mix until the yolks and whites are combined.
Preheating and Cooking: Preheat the air fryer to 390°F for three minutes with a pan inside. Pour half of the mixture into the pan and cook at 320°F for nine minutes.
Filling and Serving: Place the grated cheese on one side of the omelet. Sprinkle with chopped chives and fold it in half. Slide the omelet onto a plate and serve.

QUICHE

Servings: 4 people
Difficulty: Easy
Cooking Time: 15 minutes

Ingredients:
- 1 grated onion
- 4 eggs
- 1 Tbsp. of grated Swiss cheese
- 1 tsp. of dry mustard
- 1 cup of milk
- A pinch of black pepper

Instructions:
Preparation: Preheat the air fryer to 370°F for three minutes. Lightly spray 12 muffin tins with oil. Cut bread into circles and place them at the bottom of the muffin tins. Evenly distribute the onion and grated cheese.
Mixture and Baking: In a medium bowl, combine milk, eggs, mustard, and pepper. Pour the mixture into the tins and bake in the preheated air fryer at 370°F for 15 minutes. Check the cooking with a toothpick; if necessary, increase the cooking time by a few minutes.

POTATO FRITTATA

Servings: 2 people
Difficulty: Easy
Cooking Time: 32 minutes

Ingredients:
- 2 cups of potatoes
- 4 eggs
- 1\4 cup of milk
- 2 oz grated Parmesan cheese
- Extra virgin olive oil
- Pepper to taste
- Salt to taste

Instructions:
Potato Preparation: Peel, wash and dry the potatoes. Slice them, spray them with a bit of oil, and bake at 360°F for 14 minutes. Egg Mixture Preparation: In a bowl, beat the eggs with salt. dd milk, cheese, and pepper. Once the potatoes have cooled slightly, add them to the mixture and stir.
Cooking the Frittata: Grease a pan that fits your air fryer. Pour in the mixture and cook at 370°F for 13 minutes. With the help of a plate, turn it over and continue cooking, raising the temperature to 390°F for another five minutes.

EGGPLANTS AND CHERRY TOMATOES

Servings: 2 people
Difficulty: Easy
Cooking Time: 20 minutes

Ingredients:
- 3 eggplants
- 1 garlic clove
- Extra virgin olive oil
- 1 cup of cherry tomatoes
- A bunch of parsley
- Grana cheese flakes to taste
- Pepper to taste
- Salt to taste

Instructions:
Eggplant Preparation: Wash, dry, and trim the eggplants. Cut them in half lengthwise and make cuts on the inside. Lightly salt them. Bake at 350°F for ten minutes.
Tomato Mixture Preparation: In the meantime, wash and cut the cherry tomatoes into small pieces. Combine them in a bowl, add finely chopped garlic and parsley, salt, pepper, and oil, and let them marinate.
Filling and Final Cooking: Remove the eggplants and fill the cuts with the cherry tomatoes, being careful not to break them. Continue cooking at 360°F for another 15 minutes.
Seasoning: Season with the cherry tomato sauce and Grana cheese flakes

FAN EGGPLANTS

Servings: 2 people
Difficulty: Easy
Cooking Time: 37 minutes

Ingredients:
- 2 eggplants
- Grated Parmesan cheese
- Tomato sauce
- Extra virgin olive oil
- Cooked ham
- Emmental cheese
- Pepper to taste
- Salt to taste

Instructions:
Eggplant Preparation: Wash and trim the eggplants. Make cuts about five milimeters thick, trying not to cut all the way through, leaving the slices attached. Spray them with a bit of oil and season with a pinch of salt and pepper. Bake at 360°F for 25 minutes. Filling and Final Baking: In each slice, place a tablespoon of tomato sauce, some ham, Emmental, and some grated Parmesan cheese. Bake at 370°F for 12 minutes.

EGGPLANT CUBES

Servings: 2 people
Difficulty: Easy
Cooking Time: 18 minutes

Ingredients:
- 3 eggplants
- Extra virgin olive oil
- Salt to taste

Instructions:
Eggplant Preparation: Wash and trim the eggplants. Cut them into cubes and place them in a bowl with a handful of salt. Let them rest for about an hour.
Final Preparation and Cooking: After the time has passed, wash and squeeze the eggplant cubes. Season them with a drizzle of oil. Cook at 360°F for about 18 minutes, stirring occasionally.

BRUSCHETTA WITH EGGPLANT CREAM

Servings: 4 people
Difficulty: Easy
Cooking Time: 17 minutes

Ingredients:
- 8 slices of bread
- 2 eggplants
- 1 garlic clove
- Extra virgin olive oil
- Pepper to taste
- Salt to taste

Instructions:
Eggplant Preparation: Wash, trim, and cut the eggplants in half. Make three oblique cuts on the inside of the eggplant. Place the eggplants on the grill with the cuts facing up. Set the air fryer to 370°F for 15 minutes and cook until softened.
Cream Preparation: Once ready, extract the pulp with the help of a spoon. Blend the eggplant pulp with the garlic clove and a drizzle of oil. Season with salt and pepper.
Bruschetta Toasting: Toast the bread slices at 390°F for two minutes. Place the toasted slices on a serving plate.
Assembling and Serving: Spread the eggplant cream on the bruschetta. Serve. For a spicier taste, if desired, add some chili pepper to the eggplant cream.

RICE CROQUETTES

Servings: 15-20 croquettes
Difficulty: Easy
Cooking Time: 20 minutes

Ingredients:
- 1 2\3 cups of rice
- Saffron
- Pepper to taste
- 1 egg
- 2.8 oz grated Parmesan cheese
- Breadcrumbs
- Salt to taste

Instructions:
Rice Preparation: Wash and boil the rice. Dissolve the saffron and add it to the rice. Mix well and let it cool.
Mixing and Shaping: In a bowl, combine the rice, grated cheese, egg, salt, and pepper. Mix until the mixture is soft but compact enough to form balls. If the mixture is too thick, add one egg; if too soft, add more Parmesan or breadcrumbs.
Forming and Coating: Form balls, coat them in breadcrumbs, and place them on the air fryer grill. Spray with oil and cook at 360°F for 15-20 minutes, turning often until golden brown. Tip: Prepare the croquettes to reuse leftover risotto, or remember to make extra the next time you cook saffron risotto.

RICE CROQUETTES WITH MELTING HEART

Servings: 15-20 croquettes
Difficulty: Easy
Cooking Time: 20 minutes

Ingredients:
- 1 2\3 cups of rice
- 20 cherry-sized mozzarella balls
- Saffron
- 1 egg
- 2.8 oz grated Parmesan cheese
- Breadcrumbs
- Pepper to taste
- Salt to taste

Instructions:
Rice Preparation: Wash and boil the rice. Dissolve the saffron and add it to the rice. Mix well and let it cool.
Mixing and Shaping: In a bowl, combine the rice, grated cheese, egg, salt, and pepper. Mix until the mixture is soft but compact. Drain the mozzarella balls well, preferably letting them drain in a colander for half an hour. Take some rice, flatten it, place a mozzarella ball in the center, and close it with rice, compacting it in your hands to completely cover the mozzarella. Coating and Air Frying: Coat in breadcrumbs and place on the air fryer grill. Spray with oil and cook at 360°F for 15-20 minutes, shaking often until golden brown.
Variation: You can replace mozzarella with other cheese such as scamorza, caciocavallo, gruyere, etc.

BREADED MOZZARELLA BALLS

Servings: 20 pieces
Difficulty: Easy
Cooking Time: 15 minutes

Ingredients:
- 20 cherry-sized mozzarella balls
- Breadcrumbs
- Flour, as needed
- 2 eggs
- Extra virgin olive oil
- A pinch of salt

Instructions:
Mozzarella Preparation: Let the mozzarella balls drain for half an hour.
Coating Setup: Prepare three plates: one with flour, one with beaten eggs and a pinch of salt, and one with breadcrumbs.
Coating Process: Coat the mozzarella balls in flour, then egg then breadcrumbs. Repeat the coating process for added thickness, using only egg and breadcrumbs the second time.
Baking: Place the breaded mozzarella balls on perforated parchment paper. Spray with oil and cook at 360°F for 15 minutes.

GRATINATED MELTING CAKE

Servings: 4 people
Difficulty: Easy
Cooking Time: 20 minutes

Ingredients:
- 1 1\3 cups of risotto
- 1 oz grated Parmesan cheese
- 1 sachet of saffron
- 1\4 cup of broth or water
- 8.8 oz mozzarella
- Breadcrumbs
- 5.3 oz ham in a single slice

Instructions:
Risotto Preparation: Rinse the rice and boil it in salted water. Dissolve the saffron sachet in water or broth and add it to the rice. Mix and let it cool.
Preparing the Baking Dish: Spray a baking dish with a bit of oil. Sprinkle with some breadcrumbs and transfer half of the rice to the mold.
Filling and Baking: Slice the mozzarella and dice the ham. Place them on the rice. Cover with the remaining rice. Sprinkle with Parmesan and bake at 360°F for 20 minutes.

BAKED RICOTTA

Servings: 2 people
Difficulty: Easy
Cooking Time: 15 minutes

Ingredients:
- 2 small ricottas
- Extra virgin olive oil
- Oregano
- 20 cherry tomatoes
- Chili powder
- Salt to taste

Instructions:
Ricotta Preparation: Gently drain the ricottas and place them in a baking dish. Season with a pinch of oregano and chili powder. Bake at 360°F for ten minutes, then increase to 390°F for three minutes.
Tomato Salad Preparation: Wash, dry, and quarter the cherry tomatoes. Season with salt, oil, and oregano, and let them marinate.
Serving: Plate and serve with a drizzle of oil and the tomato salad.

GRATINATED TOMATOES

Servings: 2 people
Difficulty: Easy
Cooking Time: 15 minutes

Ingredients:
- 8 large tomatoes
- 1 bunch of parsley
- 3 Tbsp. of breadcrumbs
- 3 Tbsp. of grated Parmesan cheese
- 1 garlic clove
- Extra virgin olive oil
- Pepper
- Salt

Instructions:
Tomato Preparation: Wash and dry the tomatoes, then cut them in half. Place them in a baking dish with a drizzle of oil and lightly salt.
Breading Mixture: In a bowl, combine the ingredients for the breading: finely chop the garlic and parsley and add them to the breadcrumbs and cheese. Lightly salt and pepper. Mix with a spoon.
Gratinating: Sprinkle the breading mixture on the tomatoes. Bake at 390°F for 15 minutes.

MIXED BAKED VEGETABLES

Servings: 2 people
Difficulty: Easy
Cooking Time: 15 minutes

Ingredients:
- 1 zucchini
- 1 onion
- Pepper
- 1 bell pepper
- Extra virgin olive oil
- 1 potato
- Salt

Instructions:
Vegetable Preparation: Wash the vegetables, trim them, and cut them into cubes of the same size. Repeat the process for the potato.
Baking: Transfer everything to a baking dish. Salt and pepper the vegetables and spray with a bit of oil. Cook at 390°F for 20 minutes.

FAKE EGGPLANT BRUSCHETTA WITH HAM AND MOZZARELLA

Servings: 2 people
Difficulty: Easy
Cooking Time: 17 minutes

Ingredients:
- 3 eggplants
- 1 mozzarella
- 5.3 oz cooked ham
- Salt
- Oil

Instructions:
Eggplant Preparation: Wash, trim, and slice the eggplants about 1\4-in. thick. Spray them with oil and grill in the air fryer at 370°F for 15 minutes, turning halfway through.
Mozzarella Draining: Slice the mozzarella and let it drain in a colander.
Assembling and Final Cooking: Once the eggplants are ready, salt them on both sides. Place slices of folded ham and a slice of well-drained mozzarella on top. Return to the air fryer at 340°F for another two minutes, just enough to melt the mozzarella.

PUMPKIN AND CHEESE CRUMBLE

Servings: 8-in. diameter dish
Difficulty: Easy
Cooking Time: 60 minutes

Ingredients:
- 2 cups of cleaned pumpkin
- 5.3 oz grated Asiago cheese
- 1 onion
- 5.3 oz smoked pancetta cubes
- 2\3 cup of flour
- 1\3 cup of cold butter
- Extra virgin olive oil
- Salt to taste
- Pepper to taste

Instructions:
Pumpkin Saute: Dice the pumpkin and sauté it in a pan with oil and onion. Transfer the sautéed pumpkin to a baking dish, add half a glass of water, and set the air fryer to 360°F. Cook for 30 minutes, ensuring it does not dry out too much. Cook until softened. Once done, mash it with a fork and season with salt and pepper.
Crumble Mixture: Quickly work the flour with the cold butter to crumble it without warming it too much.
Dish Preparation: Wet and wring out parchment paper to line a 8 in. diameter dish. Pour some of the crumble into the dish and flatten it with your hands to form a base. Fill with the mashed pumpkin, a layer of pancetta cubes, and a layer of grated Asiago. Distribute the remaining crumble on top. Baking: Bake at 390°F for 30 minutes.

CAPRESE CRUMBLE

Servings: 8 in.- diameter dish
Difficulty: Easy
Cooking Time: 30 minutes

Ingredients:
- 2\3 cup of flour
- 5 basil leaves
- 1\3 cup of cold butter
- 8.8 oz mozzarella
- 3 large tomatoes
- Extra virgin olive oil
- Pepper to taste
- Salt to taste

Instructions:
Tomato and Mozzarella Preparation: Wash, dry, and slice the tomatoes. Season them in a bowl with salt, pepper, oil, and torn basil leaves. Slice the mozzarella and add it to the tomatoes.
Crumble Mixture: Quickly crumble the flour with the cold butter without warming it too much.
Dish Preparation: Wet and wring out parchment paper to line a baking dish. Pour some of the crumble into the dish and flatten it with your hands to form a base. Fill with a layer of tomatoes, a layer of mozzarella, and another layer of tomatoes. Cover with the remaining crumble.
Baking: Bake in the air fryer at 390°F for 30 minutes.

ZUCCHINI ROLLS WITH PHILADELPHIA AND SALMON

Servings: 2 people
Difficulty: Easy
Cooking Time: 9 minutes

Ingredients:
- 3 zucchinis
- 8.8 oz philadelphia cream cheese
- 1 Tbsp. of grated parmesan cheese
- 3.5 oz smoked salmon
- 2-3 chive stems
- Arugula
- Pepper to taste
- Salt to taste

Instructions:
Zucchini Preparation: Wash, trim, and slice the zucchinis into long slices approximately three milimeters thick. Spray the zucchini slices with oil and roast in the air fryer at 360°F for eight to nine minutes. Once cooked, season with another spray of oil, salt, and pepper. Cream Cheese Mixture: Wash the chives and place them in a blender with Philadelphia cheese, grated Parmesan, and smoked salmon. Blend until smooth.
Rolling and Serving: Fill the grilled zucchini slices with the blended mixture, roll them up, and serve on a plate arranged on a bed of arugula.

TUNA AND ZUCCHINI PATTIES

Servings: 2 people
Difficulty: Easy
Cooking Time: 15 minutes

Ingredients:
- 7 oz drained tuna
- Breadcrumbs, as needed
- 2 zucchinis
- 1 egg
- 8.8 oz cow's milk ricotta
- 2 Tbsp. of grated Parmesan cheese
- Garlic
- Grated zest of ½ lemon
- Salt

For the breading:
- Breadcrumbs, as needed
- 1 egg
- Extra virgin olive oil

Instructions:
Zucchini Preparation: Wash and trim the zucchinis. Grate them and place them in a bowl with a pinch of salt. Allow them to rest for about half an hour. Squeeze the grated zucchinis by hand to release excess water and place them in a bowl. Mixing Ingredients: Add the drained tuna, garlic powder, lemon zest, ricotta, grated cheese, and egg to the zucchini. Mix everything together. Gradually incorporate breadcrumbs until you achieve a soft but workable mixture.
Forming and Baking: Form meatballs from the mixture, then dip them in the egg and breadcrumbs. Spray with oil and bake at 370°F for 15 minutes.

POTATO AND CACIOCAVALLO CHEESE MEATBALLS

Servings: 2 people
Difficulty: Easy
Cooking Time: 20 minutes

Ingredients:
- 2 1\2 cups of potatoes
- 1 egg
- 1 small bunch of parsley
- 7 oz Caciocavallo cheese
- 1 garlic clove
- 1\3 cup of breadcrumbs
- Extra virgin olive oil
- Salt to taste
- Pepper to taste

Instructions:
Preparing Potatoes: Peel, dice, wash, and boil the potatoes in salted water. Drain, mash with a fork or through a vegetable mill, and place in a bowl. Season with salt and pepper, allowing them to cool slightly.
Cheese and Herb Mixture: Grate the Caciocavallo cheese and finely chop the garlic and parsley. Add them to the potatoes.
Break in the egg, add breadcrumbs, and mix everything together. Allow the mixture to rest for an hour.
Shaping and Air Frying: Take portions of the mixture, roll between your palms, and slightly flatten. Place them on the air fryer grill covered with parchment paper, spray with a bit of oil, and cook at 390°F for ten minutes. Turn them over, spray the other side, and continue cooking for another ten minutes at the same temperature.

CHEESE-CRUSTED BREAD ROLLS

Servings: 4 people
Difficulty: Easy
Cooking Time: 20 minutes

Ingredients:
- 1 pack of elongated sandwich bread
- 1 egg
- Breadcrumbs
- 5.3 oz cooked ham
- 5.3 oz spreadable cheese
- A pinch of salt
- Extra virgin olive oil

Instructions:
Preparing Bread Slices: Use a rolling pin to gently flatten the sandwich bread slices to prevent breakage during rolling.
Filling and Rolling: Spread cheese on the flattened bread slices and add ham. Roll them tightly, wrap them in plastic, and refrigerate for 30 minutes.
Egg and Breadcrumb Coating: Break the egg into a bowl, beat it with a pinch of salt, and prepare a plate with breadcrumbs. Cut the chilled bread rolls in half. Dip them in the beaten egg, coat them with breadcrumbs, and place them on the air fryer grill covered with parchment paper. Spray with oil and cook at 360°F for ten minutes. Serving Suggestion: Serve with a side of salad or grilled vegetables.

RUSTIC POTATO, MUSHROOM, AND SPECK GALETTE

Servings: 4 people
Difficulty: Easy
Cooking Time: 30 minutes

Ingredients:
- 2 rounds of puff pastry
- 1 1\3 cups of potatoes
- 5.3 oz speck
- 1 1\3 cups of mixed mushrooms or champignons
- 10.6 oz scamorza cheese
- 1 egg

For the breading:
- 3.2 oz grated Parmesan cheese
- 1 garlic clove
- Extra virgin olive oil
- Salt
- Pepper

Instructions:
Potato Preparation: Wash the potatoes and boil them in salted water for 25 minutes until they are fork-tender. Allow them to cool slightly.
Puff Pastry Handling: Retrieve the puff pastry rolls from the refrigerator.
Mushroom Saute: Clean the mushrooms, slice them, and sauté in a pan with oil and crushed garlic. Season with salt and pepper, then let them cool.
Potato Mixture: Mash the boiled potatoes and combine them with grated cheese, egg, sautéed mushrooms, julienned speck, and diced scamorza. Mix thoroughly.
Assembly and Baking: Unroll one puff pastry sheet into a baking dish lined with parchment paper. Fill with the potato mixture and cover with the second puff pastry sheet. Trim excess pastry and seal the edges with a fork. Bake at 370°F for 25-30 minutes. Serve warm.

PIZZAIOLA BISCUITS

Servings: 20 cookies
Difficulty: Easy
Cooking Time: 15 minutes

Ingredients:
- 1 1\2 cups of all-purpose flour
- 5.3 oz grated Parmesan cheese
- 1.8 oz grated Pecorino cheese
- 2\3 cup of butter
- 1\4 cup of milk
- Extra virgin olive oil, as needed
- Tomato paste, as needed
- Oregano, as needed
- Salt to taste

Instructions:
Softening Butter: Allow the butter to soften at room temperature.
Dough Preparation: In a bowl, combine cheese, flour, salt, milk, softened butter, oregano, and enough tomato paste to color the dough red. Mix thoroughly to achieve a homogeneous dough, shaping it into a ball. Wrap the dough in plastic wrap and refrigerate for approximately an hour.
Rolling and Cutting: Roll out the dough between two sheets of parchment paper. Use cookie cutters to cut out cookies. Air Frying: Place the cookies on the air fryer grill covered with perforated parchment paper. Spray with olive oil and sprinkle with oregano. Bake at 350°F for 15 minutes.

PARMESAN BISCUITS

Servings: 4 people
Difficulty: Easy
Cooking Time: 13 minutes

Ingredients:
- 2\3 cup of all-purpose flour
- Black sesame seeds
- 0.7 oz Pecorino cheese
- 0.7 fl oz milk
- 1\3 cup of cold unsalted butter
- Pistachio crumbs
- 2.8 oz grated Parmesan cheese
- A pinch of salt

Instructions:
In a bowl, swiftly combine flour, grated cheese, salt, and cold butter to prevent dough warming. Incorporate milk and knead until a ball forms. Wrap the dough in plastic and let it rest for approximately 30 minutes.
Dough Shaping: Divide the dough into two portions and shape them into logs. Roll one log in black sesame seeds and the other in pistachio crumbs. Wrap each log in parchment paper and freeze for 30 minutes to firm up. Slice the cookies to a thickness of about 1\4 of an inch and place them on perforated parchment paper.
Baking: Preheat the air fryer to 350°F. Bake the cookies for 13 minutes.

WHOLE WHEAT BREAD WITH WALNUTS

Servings: 3 loaves
Difficulty: Easy
Cooking Time: 13 minutes

Ingredients:
- 1 1\3 cups of whole wheat flour
- 1 tsp. salt
- 2\3 cup of water
- ½ tsp. sugar
- 1 tbsp of melted butter
- 1.8 oz walnut kernels
- 1 tbsp fresh yeast

Instructions:
In a glass, activate the fermentation by dissolving the yeast with sugar in some water. Let it rest for about ten minutes. In a mixer, combine whole wheat flour, softened butter, yeast mixture, and water. Start kneading, then add salt. Turn off the mixer once a ball forms and detaches from the sides. Add walnut kernels and knead for a few more seconds.
Dust a surface with flour, divide the dough into three equal parts, and shape them into loaves. Let them rise, covered, for about 2 hours or until doubled in size.
Preheat the air fryer to 390°F for five minutes.
Place the loaves on perforated parchment paper and bake at 390°F for seven minutes. Turn them over for even cooking and continue baking for another six minutes.

CEREAL BREADSTICKS

Servings: 3 breadsticks
Difficulty: Easy
Cooking Time: 13 minutes

Ingredients:
- 1 1\3 cup of cereal flour
- 1 tsp. of salt
- 3\4 cup of water
- ½ tsp. of sugar
- 1 tbsp of fresh yeast
- 1 tsp. of oil
- 1\4 cup of seeds (sesame, sunflower, chia, etc.)

Instructions:
In a glass, activate the fermentation by dissolving the yeast with sugar in some water. Let it rest for about ten minutes.
In a mixer, combine flour, dissolved yeast, oil, and the remaining water. Start kneading, then add salt. Turn off the mixer once a ball forms and detaches from the sides. Add the seeds and knead for a few more seconds.
Dust a surface with flour, divide the dough into three equal parts, and shape them into bread sticks. Make two oblique cuts on each (to monitor the rising).
Let them rise, covered until doubled in size, about two hours.
Preheat the air fryer to 390°F for five minutes.
Place the bread sticks on perforated parchment paper and bake at 390°F for seven minutes. Turn them over for even cooking and continue baking for another six minutes.

OLIVE BREAD ROLLS

Servings: 3 breadsticks
Difficulty: Easy
Cooking Time: 13 minutes

Ingredients:
- 7 oz semolina
- 1 tbsp fresh yeast
- 1\3 cup of flour
- 1 tsp. of salt
- 2\3 cup of water
- ½ tsp. of sugar
- 1 tsp. of oil
- 1\3 cup of black olives

Instructions:
Drain the olives and slice them.
Dissolve the yeast with sugar in some water in a glass. Let it rest for ten minutes until frothy.
In a mixer, combine the flour, dissolved yeast, oil, water, and olives. Mix until the dough forms a ball and detaches from the mixer's sides.
Dust a surface with some semolina, shape the dough into a log, and cut it into small pieces. Let them rise, covered, for about two hours or until doubled in size.
Preheat the air fryer to 390°F for five minutes.
Place the rolls on perforated parchment paper and bake at 390°F for eight minutes. Turn them over for even cooking and continue baking for another five minutes.

ONION BREAD ROSES

Servings: 6 roses
Difficulty: Easy
Cooking Time: 15 minutes

Ingredients:
- 1\3 cup of flour
- ½ tsp. of sugar 7 oz semolina
- 5.3 oz onions
- 2\3 cup of water
- 1 tbsp of fresh yeast
- Extra virgin olive oil
- Salt to taste

Instructions:
Thinly slice the onions and sauté them in a pan with some oil until they are well-dried. Add salt and let them cool.
Dissolve the yeast with sugar in some water. Let it rest for about ten minutes.
In a mixer, combine the flour, dissolved yeast, oil, and onions. Gradually add water while mixing. Turn off the mixer once a ball forms and detaches from the sides.
Dust a surface with semolina, shape the dough into 4 inches long and 1\3 in. thick logs, flatten them slightly with your palms, and roll them up.
Place them on perforated parchment paper, spaced apart, and let them rise until doubled in size.
Preheat the air fryer to 390°F for five minutes and bake at the same temperature for about 15 minutes.

ITALIAN-STYLE TOMATOES

Servings: 2 people
Difficulty: Easy
Cooking Time: 15 minutes

Ingredients:
- 4 large tomatoes
- 1 mozzarella
- 4 basil leaves
- Extra virgin olive oil to taste
- Salt to taste
- Pepper to taste

Instructions:
Wash and dry the tomatoes. Cut off the top while leaving the stem, and hollow them out, collecting the insides in a bowl.
Dice the mozzarella, mix it with the tomato insides, and season with salt, oil, and torn basil leaves. Place the tomatoes in an oiled baking dish, fill them with the mixture, and cover them with their tops. Bake at 350°F for seven minutes.

NEW POTATOES

Servings: 2 people
Difficulty: Easy
Cooking Time: 50 minutes

Ingredients:
- 2 cups of new potatoes
- 2 cups of coarse salt
- Extra virgin olive oil
- 2 sprigs of rosemary
- Pepper

Instructions:
Wash the potatoes thoroughly, ensuring they are of the same size for even cooking.
In a baking dish, create a thin layer of salt. Add the potatoes and rosemary, and cover them with more salt.
Bake in the air fryer at 360°F for 50 minutes.
Remove the potatoes from the basket, discarding the salt. Serve them sliced with their skin on, seasoned with pepper and extra virgin olive oil.

MILK BREAD ROLLS

Servings: 2 people
Difficulty: Medium
Cooking Time: 17 minutes

Ingredients:
- 2 cups of flour
- 1\4 cup of butter
- 1 1\2 tbsp sugar
- ½ packet of dry yeast
- 1 1\3 cup of milk
- Salt to taste

Instructions:
In a bowl, add the flour. Dissolve the yeast and sugar in the milk and add to the flour. Add the butter and knead until you get a smooth mixture. Let it rise, covered with plastic wrap, until doubled in size.
Shape the dough into balls and let them rise again until doubled.
Preheat the air fryer to 360°F for three minutes. Brush the rolls with milk and bake for two minutes at 360°F, then reduce the temperature to 320°F and bake for another 15 minutes. The number of rolls will vary based on the size you make.

BREAD SPIRALS WITH MORTADELLA AND PROVOLONE

Servings: 4 people
Difficulty: Easy
Cooking Time: 10 minutes

Ingredients:
- 4 long sandwich bread slices
- 2 eggs
- 4 slices of mortadella
- 2\3 cup of classic bagged chips
- 8 slices of provolone cheese
- 2 Tbsp. grated cheese
- 4 Tbsp. of creamy cheese

Instructions:
Lay plastic wrap on a surface and place the sandwich bread slices on it. Flatten the slices slightly with a rolling pin, spread the creamy cheese, and fill with mortadella and provolone cheese, ensuring the filling stays within the bread. Roll up the slices using the plastic wrap, wrap them tightly, and refrigerate for an hour. Break the eggs into a plate and beat them.
Crush the chips, add the grated cheese, and mix.
Unwrap the bread rolls, dip them first in the egg and then in the crushed chips, and bake at 380°F for 10 minutes. Let them cool slightly and cut into 3\4-inch thick slices to form spirals.

GORGONZOLA AND WALNUT PANZEROTTI

Servings: 4 people
Difficulty: Medium
Cooking Time: 13 minutes

Ingredients:
- 1 1\2 cups of semolina
- 2\3 cup of flour
- 1 1\4 cups of water
- ½ yeast cube
- A pinch of sugar
- 1 level tsp. of salt
- 1 tsp. oil
- For the filling:
- 5.3 oz mozzarella
- 3.5 oz gorgonzola
- 15 walnut kernels

Instructions:
Dissolve the yeast in a glass with sugar and some lukewarm water, stirring with a tsp. Let it rest for about ten minutes until a froth forms on the surface.
Pour the flour and semolina on a surface, making a well in the center.
Add the yeast, a tsp. of oil, and water to the well and start kneading. Add the salt and knead until you get a soft but not sticky dough.
Divide the dough into four balls, cover them, and let them rise in a warm place for a couple of hours.
Once risen, roll out each ball with a rolling pin on a lightly floured surface. Fill one side with mozzarella, gorgonzola, and crumbled walnut kernels.
Fold over to form a half-moon shape and seal the edges with a fork. Spray with oil and bake in the air fryer at 390°F for seven to eight minutes; turn, spray the other side, and continue baking for another five minutes.

CLASSIC PANZEROTTI

Servings: 4 people
Difficulty: Medium
Cooking Time: 13 minutes

Ingredients:
- 1 1\2 cups of semolina
- 2\3 cup of flour
- 1 1\4cups of water
- ½ yeast cube
- A pinch of sugar
- 1 level tsp. of salt
- 1 tsp. oil

For the filling:
- Tomato sauce
- 8.8 oz mozzarella
- 1 tsp. of oregano
- Olive oil to taste
- Salt to taste

Instructions:
Chop the mozzarella. If it is fresh, let it drain in a colander to remove excess moisture.
Dissolve the yeast in a glass with sugar and some lukewarm water, stirring with a tsp. Let it rest for about ten minutes until a froth forms on the surface.
Pour the flour and semolina on a surface, making a well in the center.
Add the yeast, a tsp. of oil, and water to the well and start kneading. Add the salt and knead until you get a soft but not sticky dough.
Divide the dough into four balls, cover them, and let them rise in a warm place for a couple of hours.
On a plate, season the tomato sauce with oregano, a pinch of salt, and a drizzle of olive oil.
Once risen, roll out each ball with a rolling pin on a lightly floured surface. Fill one side with some tomato sauce (keeping at least 1\3-inch from the edge) and a generous amount of mozzarella.
Fold over to form a half-moon shape and seal the edges with a fork. Spray with oil and bake at 390°F for seven to eight minutes; turn, spray the other side, and continue baking for another five minutes.

MUSHROOM AND HAM PANZEROTTI

Servings: 4 people
Difficulty: Medium
Cooking Time: 13 minutes

Ingredients:
- 1 1\3 cups of semolina
- 3\4 cup of flour
- 1 1\4 cups of water
- 1/2 yeast cube
- A pinch of sugar
- 1 level tsp. of salt

For the filling:
- 1 1\3 cups of champignon mushrooms
- 1 garlic clove
- Olive oil to taste
- Salt to taste
- 5 slices of cooked ham
- 8.8 oz mozzarella
- 1\3 cup of tomato sauce

Instructions:
Clean the mushrooms by removing the base with soil. Rinse them well and slice them.
In a pan, add a drizzle of olive oil and sauté the garlic until golden. Add the mushrooms and cook on low heat for about ten minutes. Season with salt, remove the garlic and let it cool.
In a mixer, combine the flour, yeast, water and start mixing. Add the salt and continue mixing until the dough detaches from the sides and becomes smooth.
Divide the dough into four balls, cover them, and let them rise in a warm place for a couple of hours.
Once risen, roll out each ball with a rolling pin on a lightly floured surface.
Fill one side with tomato sauce, chopped and drained mozzarella, mushrooms, and chopped ham.
Fold over to form a half-moon shape and seal the edges with a fork.
Spray with oil and bake at 390°F for seven to eight minutes; turn, spray the other side, and continue baking for another five minutes.

GRATINATED ONION

Servings: 4 people
Difficulty: Easy
Cooking Time: 20 minutes

Ingredients:
- 2 cups of giarratane onions
- 1\3 cup of breadcrumbs
- Pepper to taste
- 1 bunch of parsley
- Extra virgin olive oil
- 3 Tbsp. grated cheese
- 1 tsp. spicy paprika
- 1 Tbsp. capers
- Salt to taste

Instructions:
Peel the onions and cut them in half widthwise.
In a bowl, combine the breadcrumbs, cheese, paprika, salt, pepper, chopped parsley, and chopped capers. Add three Tbsp. of olive oil and mix until the breadcrumbs are moistened.
In a baking dish, drizzle some olive oil, place the onions, and sprinkle them with the breadcrumb mixture. Spray with oil and bake in the air fryer at 360°F for 20 minutes.

ROSE PUFF PASTRY CAKE

Servings: 4 people
Difficulty: Easy
Cooking Time: 17 minutes

Ingredients:
- 2 rectangular puff pastry rolls
- 1\3 cup of pistachio crumbs
- 5.3 oz stracchino cheese
- 1 egg yolk
- 5.3 oz mortadella
- 1 Tbsp. of milk

Instructions:
Unroll both puff pastries and spread the stracchino cheese on them.
Sprinkle with chopped pistachios and cover with mortadella.
Cut the pastry in half lengthwise and then into strips about two inches wide.
Roll them up to create roses and place them in a baking dish lined with parchment paper.
Brush them with the egg yolk beaten with a drop of milk and bake at 360°F for 17 minutes.

PUMPKIN CHIPS

Servings: 2 people
Difficulty: Easy
Cooking Time: 10 minutes

Ingredients:
- 2 cups of pumpkin
- Salt Thyme
- Pepper

Instructions:
Clean and peel the pumpkin.
Slice it thinly and place the slices in a bowl.
Season with salt, pepper, thyme, and a drizzle of olive oil. Mix well and grill at 390°F for ten minutes, shaking them often.

ROASTED CHESTNUTS

Servings: 2 people
Difficulty: Easy
Cooking Time: 20-25 minutes

Ingredients:
- 2 cups of chestnuts
- Water

Instructions:
Make a cross-cut on the chestnuts and place them in a bowl covered with water. Soak for about an hour. After soaking, drain and dry them. Bake at 360°F for 20-25 minutes.

BREADED ZUCCHINI WITH HAM AND GALBANINO

Servings: 2 people
Difficulty: Easy
Cooking Time: 22 minutes

Ingredients:
- 2 zucchinis
- 5.3 oz cooked ham
- 5.3 oz galbanino cheese
- Extra virgin olive oil

For breading:
- 1 egg
- Breadcrumbs to taste
- 2 Tbsp. of grated grana cheese

Instructions:
Wash, trim, and slice the zucchini. Spray them with oil and roast at 360°F for seven minutes. Lay them on a surface, fill them with ham and cheese, and roll them up.
Dip them in the egg and then in the breadcrumbs, then repeat the process. Place them on a grill and bake at 370°F for 15 minutes.

POTATO CUBES WITH OREGANO AND GARLIC

Servings: 2 people
Difficulty: Easy
Cooking Time: 25 minutes

Ingredients:
- 2 cups of potatoes
- 1 garlic clove
- Extra virgin olive oil
- 1 bay leaf
- 2 Tbsp. of oregano

Instructions:
Peel the potatoes and cut them into evenly sized-cubes. Soak them in cold water for about 30 minutes, then drain well and pat dry with a cloth.
Place them in a bowl with a drizzle of olive oil and season with salt, oregano, bay leaf, and finely chopped garlic. Cook at 370°F for 30 minutes, stirring often to ensure even cooking.

PUFF PASTRY WITH RICOTTA AND SALMON

Servings: 8-inch mold
Difficulty: Easy
Cooking Time: 35 minutes

Ingredients:
- 7 oz smoked salmon
- 1 roll of round puff pastry
- 1 egg
- 10.6 oz ricotta
- 1 bunch of chives

Instructions:
Take the puff pastry out of the fridge and let it sit at room temperature for about ten minutes. Meanwhile, in a bowl, combine the ricotta, smoked salmon cut into small pieces, chopped chives, and the egg. Mix all the ingredients together. Unroll the puff pastry and line the mold, leaving the parchment paper under the pastry. Pour in the filling and arrange the edges. You can either fold them over or cut and make decorations. Bake in the air fryer at 350°F for 35 minutes.

HAM PANFOCACCIA

Servings: 8-inch pan
Difficulty: Medium
Cooking Time: 30 minutes

Ingredients:
- 2\3 cup of flour
- 2\3 cup of manitoba flour
- 1 tbsp fresh yeast
- 1 tsp. of honey
- 1 tsp. salt
- 1 tbsp of olive oil
- 2\3 cup of lukewarm water
- 1\3 cup of milk

For the filling:
- 5 slices of cooked ham
- 10 slices of cheese (either Galbanino or Emmental)
- 5 Tbsp. of mayonnaise
- 3 large tomatoes
- Some lettuce leaves

Instructions:
Dissolve the yeast in a glass with honey and some water. In a mixer, add the flour, yeast, remaining water, milk, and oil. Start kneading and then add the salt. Knead for five minutes, and then place the dough in a pan lined with damp and squeezed baking paper. Let it rise for an hour.
Preheat the fryer to 390°F for three minutes and cook the pan focaccia at 350°F for 30 minutes.
Check the cooking with a toothpick. Let it cool completely, then cut it in half and spread both sides with a layer of mayonnaise. Place the pan focaccia base on a serving plate and fill it with lettuce slices, tomato slices, cooked ham, and cheese. Cover with the other half of the pan focaccia and serve.

PANFOCACCIA WITH MORTADELLA AND SPICY PROVOLONE

Servings: 8-inch pan
Difficulty: Medium
Cooking Time: 30 minutes

Ingredients:
- 2\3 cup of flour
- 2\3 cup of manitoba flour
- 1 tbsp of fresh yeast
- 1 tsp. of honey
- 1 tsp. of salt
- 1\4 cup of olive oil
- 2\3 cup of lukewarm water
- 1\3 cup of milk

For the filling:
- 5 slices of mortadella
- 7 slices of spicy provolone
- Pickled vegetables in oil
- 1 can of tuna in oil

Instructions:
Dissolve the yeast in a glass with honey and some water. In a mixer, add the flour, yeast, remaining water, milk, and oil. Start kneading and then add the salt. Knead for five minutes, and then place the dough in a pan lined with damp and squeezed baking paper. Let it rise for an hour. Preheat the fryer to 390°F for three minutes and cook the pan focaccia at 360°F for 30 minutes. Let it cool completely, and cut the pan focaccia in half. Place the base on a serving plate and fill with voluminous slices of mortadella (without laying them flat); add the drained tuna and pickled vegetables, and cover with cheese slices. Cover with the top half and serve.

STUFFED BREAD ROLLS

Servings: 15 pieces
Difficulty: Medium
Cooking Time: 16 minutes

Ingredients:
- 1\2 cup of flour
- 2\3 cup of semolina
- 2\3 cup of lukewarm water
- 1\2 tbsp of fresh yeast
- Salt to taste

For the Filling:
- 5.3 oz spicy salami
- 3.5 oz Emmentaler cheese
- 3.5 oz gorgonzola

Instructions:
In the mixer, add the flour, yeast, and water, and start the machine with the hook attachment. Add the salt and continue kneading for five minutes until you get a smooth ball. Let it rise, covered with plastic wrap, for a couple of hours. After rising, transfer the dough to a surface sprinkled with plenty of semolina and roll it out with a rolling pin to get a four milimeter thick rectangular sheet. Fill it with cheese, spicy salami, and chunks of gorgonzola. Roll the bread sheet and cut rolls about two inches long. Place them on the fryer grill with perforated baking paper and cook at 360°F for 16 minutes.

CEREAL BREAD WITH MELTING FILLING

Servings: 10 pieces
Difficulty: Medium
Cooking Time: 16 minutes

Ingredients:
- 1 cup of cereal flour
- 1 tsp. salt
- 3\4 cup of flour type 0
- 7 oz cooked ham
- 1 cup of lukewarm water
- 5.3 oz Galbanino cheese in pieces
- 1 1\2 Tbsp of olive oil
- Poppy seeds and sesame seeds for garnish
- 1\2 Tbsp of yeast
- Half a cup of milk
- 1 Tbsp. honey

Instructions:
Dissolve the yeast in some lukewarm water and honey. In the mixer bowl, combine the flour and add water, oil, and yeast. Activate the mixer with the hook attachment, add salt, and knead for ten minutes until the dough is smooth and non-sticky. Oil a bowl and place the dough inside. Cover with plastic wrap and let it rise until doubled in size. After rising, transfer the dough to a surface, shape it into a log, and cut it into pieces weighing about 2.8 oz each. Flatten them slightly and place pieces of cheese and ham in the center. Seal them well, placing the seam side down, and arrange them spaced apart on baking trays. Cover with plastic wrap and let rise for another hour. Brush with milk and sprinkle with seeds. Bake at 350°F for 16 minutes.

TRIANGULAR PASTRIES WITH TURNIP GREENS, ONION, AND GRANA CHEESE

Servings: 8 pieces
Difficulty: Medium
Cooking Time: 16 minutes

Ingredients
- 1\2 cup of flour
- 5.3 oz semolina
- 2\3 cup of lukewarm water
- 1\2 Tbsp of fresh yeast
- Salt to taste

For the Filling:
- 2 1\2 cups of turnip greens
- 1 garlic clove
- Extra virgin olive oil
- 1 hot chili pepper
- 3.5 oz Asiago cheese
- 1 onion
- 1 1\4 cups of lukewarm water
- 1\3 cup of white wine vinegar
- Salt to taste

Instructions:
Peel the onion, slice it thinly, and place it in a bowl covered with lukewarm water and vinegar. Let it marinate for about two hours. In the mixer, combine the flour, add the yeast and water, and start the machine with the hook attachment. Add salt and continue kneading for five minutes until you get a smooth ball. Let it rise, covered with plastic wrap, for a couple of hours. Blanch the turnip greens in unsalted water until soft. In a pan, heat some oil and add crushed garlic and finely chopped chili pepper. Add the turnip greens and sauté for five minutes; season with salt, let it cool and remove the garlic. Drain the onion and dice the Asiago cheese. After the dough has risen, transfer it to a surface sprinkled with semolina and roll it out into a rectangular sheet about 0.1-0.2 inch thick. Cut into three to four inches squares and fill one corner with turnip greens, Asiago cheese cubes, and onion. Fold to form a triangle, sealing the edges well, and bake at 360°F for 17 minutes.

SAVORY CAKE WITH MUSHROOMS, POTATOES, SPECK, AND BRIE

Servings: 4 people
Difficulty: Easy
Cooking Time: 30 minutes

Ingredients:
- 1 roll of brisee dough
- Pepper to taste
- 3 potatoes
- Extra virgin olive oil
- 1 cup of champignon mushrooms
- A bunch of parsley
- 1 garlic clove
- 5.3 oz Brie cheese
- Salt to taste

Instructions:
Wash, peel, and boil the potatoes. Cook until they are soft when pierced with a fork.
Clean and slice the champignons. Sauté them in a pan with a drizzle of oil and the garlic clove. Cook for about ten minutes on low heat, covered. Remove the garlic and let it cool.
Drain the potatoes and mash them with a fork. Add the mushrooms, season with salt and pepper, add the Brie cheese cut into small pieces, and finely chopped parsley. Mix everything together.
Unroll the brisee dough and fill it with the mixture. Bake at 360°F for 35 minutes.

FAKE PUMPKIN OMELETTE

Servings: 4 people
Difficulty: Easy
Cooking Time: 30 minutes

Ingredients:
- 1 cup of pumpkin
- 1 egg
- 1 cup of flour
- 1 onion
- 1 1\4 cups of water
- 3 Tbsp. of breadcrumbs
- 1 Tbsp. of salt
- 3 Tbsp. of grated parmesan cheese
- 1 sprig of rosemary
- Extra virgin olive oil

Instructions:
Peel the pumpkin, remove the seeds and fibers, and cut it into small cubes. Also, clean the onion and finely chop it. In a bowl, beat the egg, add salt, flour, water, and mix. You will get a soft batter. Add the pumpkin, onion, and rosemary (deprived of the woody part). Mix everything and pour it into a baking pan lined with parchment paper. Sprinkle with breadcrumbs and parmesan cheese, drizzle with oil, and bake in the air fryer at 390°F for 30 minutes.

ZUCCHINI ROLLS CAPRESE STYLE

Servings: 4 people
Difficulty: Easy
Cooking Time: 8 minutes

Ingredients:
- 3 zucchinis
- 2\3 cup of cherry tomatoes
- 7 oz mozzarella cheese
- 3 basil leaves
- Extra virgin olive oil
- Pepper to taste
- Salt to taste

Instructions:
Wash the cherry tomatoes and cut them into small pieces. Season with salt, pepper, and oil. Mix and add the mozzarella cheese cut into small pieces and hand-torn basil leaves. Let it marinate for about an hour.
Meanwhile, wash, trim, and thinly slice the zucchini. Spray them with oil and grill in your air fryer at 380°F for eight minutes, turning halfway through.
Once all the zucchinis are cooked, place them on a work surface, season with salt and pepper, and add a generous spoonful of Caprese filling to each slice. Roll them up, ensuring the seam is at the bottom. Drizzle with some fresh olive oil and serve.

CAULIFLOWER GRATIN

Servings: 4 people
Difficulty: Easy
Cooking Time: 20 minutes

Ingredients:
- 1 small cauliflower
- 1 egg
- 3.5 oz pancetta
- 1\3 cup of vinegar
- 3.5 oz speck
- 1\3 cup of bread crumbs
- 3.5 oz Emmental cheese
- 3.5 oz smoked scamorza cheese
- 3.5 oz grated cheese
- Extra virgin olive oil
- A bunch of parsley
- Garlic powder to taste
- Chili pepper to taste
- Pepper to taste
- Salt to taste

Instructions:
Clean the cauliflower by removing the leaves and cutting the florets.
Boil the florets in salted boiling water with vinegar and cook for about 15 minutes. Then drain well and let it cool.
In a small bowl, beat the egg with a pinch of salt. In another bowl, combine the bread crumbs, finely chopped parsley, half of the cheese, garlic powder, and chili pepper. Dice the speck, pancetta, Emmental, and scamorza.
Dip the florets first in the egg and then in the breadcrumbs. Place them in a baking dish with a drizzle of oil. Arrange them next to each other and top with cubes of cheese, speck, and pancetta, the remaining grated cheese, and a drizzle of oil. Bake at 360°F for 20 minutes.

POTATOES PIZZAIOLA STYLE

Servings: 4 people
Difficulty: Easy
Cooking Time: 15 minutes

Ingredients:
- 3 potatoes
- 1 1\4 cups of tomato sauce
- Extra virgin olive oil
- 1 garlic clove
- 8.8 oz mozzarella
- Oregano to taste

Instructions:
Wash the potatoes well and place them in a pan. Cover with cold water and bring to a boil. Boil the potatoes for about 15-20 minutes (cooking time varies depending on the size of the potatoes).
Meanwhile, prepare the sauce by heating some oil in a pan, adding the garlic clove, and after a minute, add the tomato sauce. Cook for about 10-15 minutes. Season with salt, add some oregano and let it cool.
Drain the potatoes, let them cool, then peel and slice them.
Drizzle some oil in a baking dish and layer the potato slices, cover with tomato sauce, add mozzarella, and continue layering until all ingredients are used up. Bake at 350°F for 15 minutes.

POTATOES WITH STRACCHINO CHEESE AND MORTADELLA

Servings: 2 people
Difficulty: Easy
Cooking Time: 15 minutes

Ingredients:
- 3 potatoes
- 2 Tbsp. of breadcrumbs
- 10.6 oz mortadella
- 2 Tbsp. of grated parmesan cheese
- 7 oz stracchino cheese

Instructions:
Wash the potatoes well and place them in a pan. Cover with cold water and bring to a boil. Boil the potatoes for about 15-20 minutes (cooking time varies depending on the size of the potatoes).
Drain the potatoes, let them cool, then peel and slice them.
Drizzle some oil in a baking dish and layer the potato slices; add some stracchino cheese and mortadella cubes. Continue layering until all ingredients are used up, finishing with potatoes, stracchino, breadcrumbs, and grated cheese. Bake at 350°F for 15 minutes.

POTATOES WITH GORGONZOLA, SPECK, AND WALNUTS

Servings: 2 people
Difficulty: Easy
Cooking Time: 15 minutes

Ingredients:
- 2 potatoes
- 3.5 oz speck
- 10.6 oz gorgonzola cheese
- 2 Tbsp. of breadcrumbs
- 3\4 cup of walnut kernels
- 2 Tbsp. of grated Parmesan cheese

Instructions:
Wash the potatoes well and place them in a pan. Cover with cold water and bring to a boil. Boil the potatoes for about 15-20 minutes (cooking time varies depending on the size of the potatoes). Check the doneness by piercing with a fork.
Drain the potatoes, let them cool, then peel and slice them. Chop the walnut kernels.
Drizzle some oil in a baking dish and layer the potato slices; add gorgonzola cheese and walnut kernels. Continue layering until all ingredients are used up, finishing with potatoes, gorgonzola, breadcrumbs, and grated cheese. Bake at 350°F for 15 minutes.

GORGONZOLA AND CARAMELIZED ONION BASKETS

Servings: 2 people
Difficulty: Easy
Cooking Time: 8 minutes

Ingredients:
- 6 slices of bread
- 1\3 cup of white wine vinegar
- 1 1\3 cups of red onion
- 2 Tbsp. of sugar
- Extra virgin olive oil
- Salt to taste

Instructions:
Flatten the bread slices slightly with a rolling pin so they can be molded without breaking.
Use individual aluminum molds, turn them upside down, and shape the bread slices over them to create a small bowl. Spray some oil and bake at 350°F for eight minutes.
In a pan, heat some oil and cook the onion for five minutes, stirring often. Then add half a glass of water and continue cooking covered for another ten minutes.
After ten minutes, reduce the heat to low and add vinegar and sugar. Mix and let it evaporate for another three-four minutes. Season with salt and let it cool.
Serve the caramelized onions in the bread bowls, adding the onions just before serving to prevent the bowls from getting soggy and breaking.

POTATOES AND ROSEMARY

Servings: 2 people
Difficulty: Easy
Cooking Time: 8 minutes

Ingredients:
- 2 potatoes
- Pepper to taste
- 3 sprigs of rosemary
- Extra virgin olive oil
- Garlic powder
- Salt to taste

Instructions:
Wash the potatoes well and place them in a pan. Cover with cold water and bring to a boil. Boil the potatoes for about 15 minutes (cooking time varies depending on the size of the potatoes).
Let the potatoes cool, then peel and slice them.
In a baking dish, drizzle some oil at the base, layer the potato slices, season with salt, pepper, and garlic powder, and sprinkle with rosemary. Cover with the remaining potato slices and season again with salt, pepper, garlic powder, and rosemary sprigs. Finish with a drizzle of oil and bake at 360°F for 30 minutes.

EGGPLANT BRISE TART

Servings: 4 people
Difficulty: Easy
Cooking Time: 15 minutes

Ingredients:
- 1 roll of shortcrust pastry
- 3.5 oz smoked scamorza cheese
- 2 small eggplants
- 6 cherry tomatoes
- 1 garlic clove
- Extra virgin olive oil

Instructions:
Wash and dice the eggplants.
In a pan with some oil, sauté the garlic, add the eggplants, and cook on low heat with a lid for about ten minutes. Season with salt and add the washed and quartered cherry tomatoes. Cook for another five minutes, then turn off the heat and let it cool. Remove the garlic.
Unroll the Brise pastry and line a baking dish, trimming any excess.
Add finely chopped scamorza cheese to the eggplants and pour the mixture into the brise pastry. Use the trimmings to form the typical tart strips.
Bake at 380°F for 15 minutes.

BRISE TART WITH EGGPLANT AND SAUSAGE

Servings: 4 people
Difficulty: Easy
Cooking Time: 15 minutes

Ingredients:
- 2 rolls of shortcrust pastry
- 1 garlic clove
- 2 small eggplants
- 6 cherry tomatoes
- 3 sausage links
- Extra virgin olive oil

Instructions:
Wash and dice the eggplants.
In a pan with some oil, sauté the garlic, add the eggplants, and cook on low heat with a lid for about ten minutes. Season with salt and add the washed and quartered cherry tomatoes. Cook for another five minutes, then turn off the heat and let it cool. Remove the garlic.
Remove the casing from the sausage, crumble it, and add it to the eggplants.
Unroll one Brise pastry and line a baking dish. Fill with the mixture and cover with the other pastry. Bake in the air fryer at 380°F for 15 minutes.

PUMPKIN SAVORY CAKE

Servings: 2 people
Difficulty: Easy
Cooking Time: 30 minutes

Ingredients:
- 1 cup of pumpkin
- 2 Tbsp. of pecorino cheese
- 3\4 cup of flour
- 3 Tbsp. of grated parmesan cheese
- 1 1\4 cups of water
- 1 egg
- 2 tsp of sea salt
- 1 onion
- 1 sprig of rosemary

Instructions:
Clean the pumpkin and cut it into small cubes.
Grease a sheet of parchment paper with oil spray and line a baking dish; pour in the pumpkin cubes.
Clean and thinly slice the onion and place it on the pumpkin; garnish with finely chopped rosemary needles.
In a bowl, break the egg, add water, salt, flour, and cheese, and mix everything. Pour the mixture over the pumpkin and bake at 390°F for 30 minutes.

QUICK STUFFED DANUBE

Servings: 2 people
Difficulty: Easy
Cooking Time: 20 minutes

Ingredients:
- 1 rectangular roll of shortcrust pastry
- 4.2 oz Emmental cheese cubes
- 4.2 oz cooked ham
- Half cup of milk

Instructions:
Take the brisee out of the fridge at least ten minutes before using it.
Chop the cooked ham together with the cheese.
Unroll the Brisee and divide it into 3x3 in. squares. For each square, place some ham and cheese in the center and close by joining all the edges to form a ball.
Place a sheet of parchment paper inside a baking dish, place the balls slightly spaced apart, and let them rise in the dish for another hour.
Brush the balls with a little milk and bake at 360°F for ten minutes, then increase to 370°F and bake for another ten minutes.

SALAMI RING CAKE WITHOUT LEAVENING

Servings: 7.9 in- ring mold
Difficulty: Easy
Cooking Time: 25 minutes

Ingredients:
- 2\3 cup of milk
- 3.5 oz salami
- 1\4 cup of sunflower seed oil
- 4.4 oz provolone cheese
- 2 eggs
- 2 Tbsp. of butter
- 1\3 cup of sun-dried tomatoes
- 3.5 oz grated parmesan cheese
- 1\4 cup of black olives
- 1 sachet of instant yeast
- 1 cup of flour
- Salt to taste
- Pepper to taste

Instructions:
Butter and flour the ring mold.
Dice the salami, provolone, and sun-dried tomatoes, and slice the olives.
In a mixer, add flour, yeast, cheese, salt, and pepper and mix. Add eggs, oil, and milk and mix again until you get a smooth and homogeneous mixture.
Add the salami, provolone, sun-dried tomatoes, and olives to the mixture and mix well. Pour the mixture into the mold and bake at 360°F for 25-30 minutes.
Do the toothpick test to check if it's cooked. Let it cool and serve.

VEGETABLE RING CAKE WITHOUT LEAVENING

Servings: 8 in. ring mold
Difficulty: Easy
Cooking Time: 25 minutes

Ingredients:
- 1 cup of flour
- 2 Tbsp. butter
- 3\4 cup of milk
- ½ yellow bell pepper
- 1\4 cup of sunflower seed oil
- ½ red bell pepper
- 2 eggs
- 1\3 cup of sun-dried tomatoes
- 3.5 oz grated parmesan cheese
- 1 zucchini
- 1 sachet of instant yeast
- Pepper to taste
- Salt to taste

Instructions:
Butter and flour the ring mold.
Wash the vegetables; trim the zucchini and cut them into cubes while slicing the bell peppers and sun-dried tomatoes into strips. In a mixer, add flour, yeast, cheese, salt, and pepper and mix. Add eggs, oil, and milk and mix again until you get a smooth and homogeneous mixture.
Add the vegetables to the mixture and mix well. Pour the mixture into the mold and cook in the air fryer at 360°F for 25-30 minutes. Do the toothpick test to check if it's cooked. Let it cool and serve.

MINTED ZUCCHINI

Servings: 2
Difficulty: Medium
Cooking Time: 8 minutes

Ingredients:
- 2 zucchinis
- Pepper, to taste
- Extra virgin olive oil to taste
- 1 garlic clove
- 2-3 sprigs of mint
- Salt to taste

Instructions:
Wash, trim the zucchinis, and slice them. Spray with olive oil and grill at 390°F for eight minutes, stirring halfway through for even cooking.

Finely chop the garlic and place it in a small bowl; tear the mint with your hands and transfer the zucchini to a plate. Season with salt, pepper, and olive oil. Let it sit for a while before serving.

FIRST COURSES

MUSHROOM AND SAUSAGE CREPES

Servings: 4
Difficulty: High
Cooking Time: 20 minutes

Ingredients:
For the Crepes:
- 1 cup of milk
- 1 egg
- ¾ cup of flour
- A pinch of salt
- 2 Tbsp. of butter
- For the Filling:
- 1 garlic clove
- 10.5 oz sausage
- 1 cup of champignon mushrooms
- 7 oz smoked scamorza cheese

Béchamel sauce:
- 2 1\2 Tbsp. of butter
- ⅓ cup of flour
- 1⅔ cups of milk
- ¼ cup of grated cheese for sprinkling
- Salt, to taste
- Pepper, to taste
- Nutmeg, to taste

Instructions:
For the crepes: Beat the eggs in a bowl with a pinch of salt, add the flour, some milk, and the melted and cooled butter. Mix and add the remaining flour. Let the mixture rest for 30 minutes.

Meanwhile, clean and slice the mushrooms and place them in the air fryer with a garlic clove and crumbled sausage. Cook at 360°F for 15 minutes, stirring occasionally.

Prepare the béchamel sauce by melting the butter in a saucepan, adding the flour gradually to avoid lumps, then gradually add the milk. Stir until it thickens slightly. Season with salt, pepper, and nutmeg.

Heat a crepe pan, grease it with some butter, and cook the crepes by quickly rotating the pan. (This dose will yield about eight crepes with a diameter of 11 inches.)

Mix the sausage and mushrooms with a couple of Tbsp. of béchamel and a generous Tbsp. of grated cheese. Fill the crepes with the mixture, fold them into quarters, and place them in a baking dish where you've spread some béchamel.

Top the crepes with the remaining béchamel and sprinkle with cheese. Bake in the air fryer at 370°F for ten minutes.

MELTING RICE FRITTATA

Servings: 4
Difficulty: Low
Airfryer Cooking Time: 12 minutes

Ingredients:
- 1 3\4 cups of rice
- 1½ cups of tomato sauce
- ¼ cup of grated parmesan cheese
- 7 oz mozzarella

Instructions:
Prepare Rice: Boil the rice in salted water, draining it a few minutes earlier than the time indicated on the package.
Mix Ingredients: In a large bowl, combine the rice with the tomato sauce and grated cheese.
Prepare Airfryer Pan: Drizzle some oil on the airfryer pan and sprinkle with breadcrumbs on both the bottom and sides. Layer and Bake: Pour half of the rice mixture into the pan, layer with sliced mozzarella, and cover with the remaining rice, pressing slightly to compact it. Top with more tomato sauce and sprinkle with Parmesan. Bake at 360°F for ten minutes, then increase the temperature to 390°F for the last two minutes.

PENNE WITH ARTICHOKES AND SAUSAGE

Servings: 2
Difficulty: Low
Airfryer Cooking Time: 27 minutes

Ingredients:
- Béchamel Sauce
- 1 1\3 cups of penne
- 2.5 Tbsp. of butter
- 3 artichokes
- ⅓ cup of flour
- 7 oz sausage
- 3.5 oz smoked scamorza cheese
- 1⅔ cups of milk
- ¼ cup of grated cheese
- Salt, to taste
- Pepper, to taste
- Grated nutmeg, to taste

Instructions:
Prepare Pasta: Boil the pasta in salted water and drain it while still al dente (two minutes before the usual cooking time). Prep Artichokes and Sausage: Clean the artichokes and place them in a bowl with water and the juice of half a lemon. Slice them, drain, and place them in the air fryer pan with the garlic clove. Add crumbled sausage and cook at 360°F for 15 minutes, stirring occasionally.
Make Béchamel Sauce: Meanwhile, prepare the béchamel sauce as described above.
Combine Ingredients: In a bowl, combine the pasta with some béchamel and the sausage with artichokes, setting some aside. In an air fryer pan, spread some béchamel at the base, layer with pasta and smoked scamorza cheese, and sprinkle with Parmesan. Repeat the layers and sprinkle with Parmesan on top.
Bake: Pour some water around the edges, if necessary, to prevent drying during cooking. Bake at 390°F for 12 minutes.

BAKED LASAGNA WITH "FRIED" EGGPLANT

Servings: 2
Difficulty: Low
Airfryer Cooking Time: 28-33 minutes

Ingredients:
- 4 oz. of lasagna sheets
- 1 eggplant
- Sliced smoked scamorza cheese
- 8.8 oz ground veal
- 1 mozzarella
- Basil
- Grated Parmesan cheese
- Tomato sauce
- Cooking oil, for frying
- Onion
- Salt

Instructions:
Prepare Eggplant: Wash, dry, and trim the eggplant. Slice it thinly and sprinkle with salt. Place it in a colander, cover it with a plate, and weigh it down to drain for about an hour. Make Tomato Sauce: In a pot, prepare the sauce by finely chopping the onion with some olive oil. Add the ground veal and sauté. Add the tomato sauce and cook on low heat for about an hour. Season with salt and, once off the heat, add basil leaves and let it rest. Airfry Eggplant: Take the eggplant slices, rinse them, squeeze out excess water, quickly pass them in some oil, and cook in the airfryer at 390°F for three minutes on each side. Lightly salt and set aside. Assemble Lasagna: In an air fryer pan, spread a ladle of sauce diluted with a little water. Alternate layers of pasta, shredded mozzarella,
Parmesan, smoked scamorza, and eggplant, and cover with sauce. Repeat until all ingredients are used up, finishing with sauce and a generous sprinkle of Parmesan. Bake: Pour a little water around the edges to prevent drying during cooking. Bake at 390°F for 25-30 minutes. Check the cooking with a fork; it should be soft. Let it rest for about ten minutes before serving.

PENNE WITH CHICKEN AND BELL PEPPERS

Servings: 2
Difficulty: Low
Cooking Time: 15 minutes

Ingredients:
- Olive oil, to taste
- 10.5 oz chicken breast
- ½ cup of white wine
- 1 yellow bell pepper
- 1 Tbsp. of capers
- 1 red bell pepper
- 1\4 cup of pitted black olives
- 1 garlic clove
- 1 cup of penne pasta

Instructions:
Prepare Chicken and Vegetables: Dice the chicken breast and slice the bell peppers into strips. Finely chop the garlic and place everything in an air fryer pan. Cook in Airfryer: Add some olive oil and wine and cook at 390°F for ten minutes, stirring occasionally. Add capers and black olives and continue cooking for another five minutes. Cook Penne: Meanwhile, boil the penne in salted water. Once cooked, drain and transfer to a bowl. Combine and Serve: Add the chicken and bell pepper mixture to the penne. Mix well before serving.

MACARONI WITH CAULIFLOWER AND BACON

Servings: 2
Difficulty: Low
Airfryer Cooking Time: 27 minutes

Ingredients:
- 3\4 cup of macaroni
- ½ cup of white wine
- 1 1\3 cups of cauliflower
- 1 garlic clove
- 3.5 oz pork bacon
- 2.8 oz grated Pecorino cheese
- 2 tbsp. of olive oil
- Salt, to taste
- Pepper, to taste

Instructions:
Prepare Vegetables and Pasta: Clean the cauliflower and cut it into florets. Boil in salted water. After about three minutes, add the macaroni and cook everything, draining three minutes earlier than the usual cooking time.
Drain and Season: Drain and transfer to a bowl, adding a drizzle of olive oil to prevent the pasta from sticking. In a small bowl, combine the two types of grated cheese and add half to the pasta. Mix well.
Prepare Airfryer Pan: Grease an airfryer pan with some butter, sprinkle half of the breadcrumbs, and add the pasta.
Top and Bake: Top with the remaining breadcrumbs and cheese. Add a few butter flakes and bake at 360°F for 13 minutes, then increase to 390°F for another five minutes.

MACARONI WITH BROCCOLI, CAULIFLOWER, AND GRATIN

Servings: 2
Difficulty: Low
Airfryer Cooking Time: 18 minutes

Ingredients:
- 1.4 oz grated Parmesan cheese
- 2\3 cup of macaroni
- 1\4 cup of breadcrumbs
- 2\3 cup of cauliflower
- 1 garlic clove
- 2\3 cup of romanesco broccoli
- 3.5 oz diced smoked scamorza cheese
- 2.8 oz grated Pecorino cheese
- A few butterflakes
- Pepper, to taste
- Salt, to taste

Instructions:
Prepare Vegetables and Pasta: Clean the broccoli and cauliflower, cut into florets, and boil in salted water. After about three minutes, add the macaroni and cook everything, draining three minutes earlier than the usual cooking time.
Drain and Season: Drain and transfer to a bowl, adding a drizzle of olive oil to prevent the pasta from sticking. In a small bowl, combine the two types of grated cheese and add half to the pasta. Mix well.
Prepare Airfryer Pan: Grease an airfryer pan with some butter, sprinkle half of the breadcrumbs, and add the pasta.
Top and Bake: Top with the remaining breadcrumbs and cheese. Add a few butter flakes and bake at 360°F for 13 minutes, then increase to 390°F for another five minutes.

TROFIETTE WITH PUMPKIN CREAM

Servings: 4
Difficulty: Low
Airfryer Cooking Time: 30 minutes

Ingredients:
- 1 1\3 cups of milk
- 1 1\2 cups of pumpkin
- 3.5 oz scamorza cheese
- 1 cup of trofiette pasta
- 1\8 cup of flour
- 1 oz grated parmesan cheese
- 7 oz sausage
- 1\8 cup of butter
- Pepper, to taste
- Salt, to taste
- Nutmeg, to taste

Instructions:
Prepare Pumpkin: Clean the pumpkin, removing the skin, seeds, and fibers. Slice, spray with a bit of oil, and cook in the air fryer at 360°F for 14-15 minutes. Check for doneness with a skewer.
Make Béchamel Sauce: In a pot, prepare the béchamel sauce: melt the butter, add the flour and milk, and stir until cooked. Season with salt, pepper, and a dash of nutmeg.
Prepare Sausage: Remove the sausage casing, crumble, and lightly brown at 390°F for five minutes.
Blend Pumpkin: Dice the scamorza cheese and blend the pumpkin with the béchamel.
Cook Pasta: Boil the pasta in salted water, draining it three minutes earlier than usual.
Assemble and Bake: Season the pasta with a generous ladle of béchamel, some scamorza, and all the sausage. Mix everything and transfer to a baking dish. Cover with the remaining scamorza, béchamel, and grated cheese. Bake at 390°F for ten minutes.

ORECCHIETTE WITH TOMATO AND MOZZARELLA GRATIN

Servings: 4
Difficulty: Low
Airfryer Cooking Time: 10 minutes

Ingredients:
- 1 cup of orecchiette pasta
- 8.8 oz mozzarella
- 3 basil leaves
- 2 cups of tomatoes
- 3.5 oz parmesan cheese
- 1 small onion
- 7 oz cheese of choice (Cheddar, Fontina, Scamorza, Emmental, etc.)
- Olive oil, to taste

Instructions:
Prepare Tomato Sauce: In a pan with some olive oil, add halved tomatoes and roughly chopped onion. Cook on low heat for 15 minutes with a lid. Pass the tomatoes through a food mill to remove skins and seeds. Return to the pan and cook on very low heat for another five minutes with the lid slightly ajar. Turn off the heat, season with salt, and add rinsed and dried basil leaves. Let it rest.
Cook Orecchiette: Meanwhile, cook the orecchiette in salted water until al dente.
Prepare Cheese: Dice the cheese.
Assemble and Bake: Season the pasta with a generous ladle of tomato sauce and some diced cheese. Place half of the pasta in a baking dish, add a layer of cheese, and cover with a generous ladle of fresh tomato sauce. Repeat the layers, finishing with sauce and cheese on top. Bake at 370°F for ten minutes.
Note: You can also use individual terracotta containers. For the sauce, you can use different types of tomatoes or mix them, e.g., yellow and red cherry tomatoes, Piccadilly, San Marzano, cluster tomatoes, etc.

RICE-STUFFED TOMATOES

Servings: 4
Difficulty: Low
Airfryer Cooking Time: 20 minutes

Ingredients:
- 4 large round red tomatoes
- 3.5 oz grated parmesan cheese
- 1 garlic clove
- 7 oz arborio rice
- Parsley
- Salt, to taste
- Olive oil, to taste

Instructions:
Prepare Tomatoes: Wash and dry the tomatoes. Cut off the top ⅔ to create lids. Scoop out the pulp with a spoon. Place the tomatoes upside down to drain.
Prepare Rice Mixture: Blend the tomato pulp with parsley and garlic. Add the well-rinsed rice, mix, and let it rest for about an hour.
Grease Baking Dish: Grease the baking dish with olive oil.
Fill and Cook Tomatoes: Fill the tomatoes with the rice mixture, cover them with their lids, and place them in the dish. Cook in the air fryer at 360°F for 15 minutes, then increase to 390°F for another five minutes.

BREAD MEATBALL-STUFFED TOMATOES

Servings: 4
Difficulty: Medium
Airfryer Cooking Time: 15 minutes

Ingredients:
- 4 large round red tomatoes
- 1 garlic clove
- 1\3 cup of breadcrumbs
- 3.5 oz grated Parmesan cheese
- 2 eggs
- Parsley
- Salt, to taste
- Olive oil, to taste

Instructions:
Prepare Tomatoes: Wash and dry the tomatoes, keeping the stem. Cut off the top ⅔ to create lids. Scoop out the pulp with a spoon. Place the tomatoes upside down to drain.
Prepare Filling: In a bowl, combine breadcrumbs, eggs, cheese, finely chopped parsley, and garlic. Mix well.
Grease Baking Dish: Grease the baking dish with olive oil.
Fill and Bake Tomatoes: Fill the tomatoes with the mixture, sprinkle with the remaining cheese, and bake at 370°F for 15 minutes.

STUFFED ZUCCHINI WITH RICE

Servings: 4
Difficulty: Medium-High
Airfryer Cooking Time: 15 minutes

Ingredients:
- 8 round zucchinis
- 7 oz Emmental cheese (or Galbanino, Cheddar)
- 3.5 oz grated Parmesan cheese
- 3\4 cup of rice
- 10.6 oz shrimp
- 1 garlic clove
- 2 eggs
- Olive oil, to taste
- Salt, to taste

Instructions:
Prepare Zucchinis: Wash and dry the zucchinis. Cut off the top tagliatella nests ⅔ to create lids. Scoop out the pulp with a spoon.
Briefly blanch the zucchinis and their lids and let them cool.
Sauté Zucchini Pulp: Chop the zucchini pulp and sauté with a bit of oil and crushed garlic. Add the peeled shrimp heads and cook for five minutes on very low heat. Remove the garlic.
Boil Rice: Meanwhile, boil the rice in salted water and drain.
Prepare Filling: In a bowl, combine the zucchini pulp, shrimp, eggs, most of the cheese (reserve some for topping), and rice. Mix well.
Fill and Bake Zucchinis: Fill the zucchinis with the mixture, sprinkle with the remaining cheese, and bake at 370°F for 15 minutes.

ZUCCHINI WITH COUSCOUS AND SHRIMP

Servings: 4
Difficulty: Medium-High
Airfryer Cooking Time: 15 minutes

Ingredients:
- 4 long zucchinis
- 3\4 cup of couscous
- 10.6 oz shrimp
- 2 eggs
- 3.5 oz grated parmesan cheese
- 7 oz mild provolone cheese
- 1 garlic clove
- Olive oil, to taste
- Salt, to taste

For the Shrimp Broth:
- Shrimp heads
- 1 small onion
- Olive oil
- A bunch of parsley
- 1 garlic clove
- ⅛ cup white wine

Instructions:
Prepare Shrimp Broth: Wash the shrimp, remove the heads, and peel. In a pot, heat some oil, add crushed garlic and roughly chopped onion. Sauté for two minutes, add shrimp heads and cook for another two minutes. Deglaze with white wine, and add parsley and water. Bring to a boil, making a broth. Cook for 30-40 minutes on low heat, skimming off any foam. Press the shrimp heads with a fork to release more flavor. Taste and adjust seasoning. Strain the broth, measuring out 0.85 cup, and add the couscous to it. Cover and let it hydrate.
Prepare Zucchinis: Wash, trim, and slice the zucchinis lengthwise. Scoop out the pulp, being careful not to break them. Chop the zucchini pulp and sauté with a bit of oil and crushed garlic. Add the peeled shrimp and cook for five minutes on very low heat. Remove the garlic. Briefly blanch the zucchinis, drain, and let them cool.
Prepare Couscous Mixture: Fluff the couscous and transfer to a bowl. Add the zucchini pulp, shrimp, eggs, and most of the cheese (reserve some for topping). Mix well.
Fill and Bake Zucchinis: Fill the zucchinis with the mixture, sprinkle with the remaining cheese, and bake at 370°F for 15 minutes.

RICE WITH POTATOES AND MUSSELS

Servings: 4
Difficulty: High
Airfryer Cooking Time: 45 minutes

Ingredients:
- 3\4 cup of Arborio rice
- 2.2 lb. mussels
- 1.1 lb. yellow-fleshed potatoes
- A bunch of parsley
- 2\3 cup of golden onions
- 2 garlic cloves
- Breadcrumbs
- 1 1\3 cups of ripe tomatoes
- 3.5 oz Pecorino cheese
- Extra virgin olive oil
- Salt, to taste
- Pepper, to taste

Instructions:
Prepare Mussels: Clean the mussels by removing the beard and scraping the surface with another mussel's back. Wash them well under running water and soak them in cold water. To open the mussels raw, slide the valves against each other, insert a small knife to open them, and keep the mussel on one shell while discarding the other. Set aside.
Alternative Mussel Opening: For a quicker method, sauté garlic with some oil and parsley in a large pan. Add the mussels and cook on high heat with the lid on, shaking occasionally, until they open (about three-four minutes). Remove the mussel from the shell that it's not attached to. Strain the mussel water to remove any sand or shell residues. Mix with some water and set aside. Prepare Rice and Potatoes: Soak the rice in cold water. Wash, peel, and slice the potatoes into three to four milimeter slices. Soak in cold water with a pinch of salt.
Prepare Onion and Tomato Mixture: Peel and thinly slice the onions. Mix with sliced tomatoes season with oil and salt.
Prepare Parsley, Garlic, and Pecorino Mixture: In another bowl, combine finely chopped parsley, garlic, and Pecorino cheese.
Season Potatoes: Drain the potatoes, dry them, and season with oil, salt, and pepper. Rinse the rice under water.
Assemble Dish: Oil a baking dish and layer with onions and tomatoes, followed by potatoes, more onions and tomatoes, mussels, and rice. Top with the Pecorino mixture, more onions, tomatoes, and potatoes.
Add Mussel Water: Pour over the diluted mussel water until it reaches the potato level. Sprinkle with Pecorino and breadcrumbs.
Bake: Bake at 370°F for 40 minutes, then increase to 390°F for another five minutes. The dish is ready when the potatoes form a golden crust, and the liquid has evaporated.

CLASSIC BAKED PASTA

Servings: 2
Difficulty: Low
Cooking Time: 15 minutes

Ingredients:
- 1 cup of macaroni
- 1 small celery stalk
- 5.3 oz ground veal
- 1 mozzarella
- 2\3 cup of tomato sauce
- 3.5 oz grated Parmesan cheese
- ½ onion
- Extra virgin olive oil
- ½ carrot

Instructions:
Prepare Vegetables: Finely chop the onion, celery, and carrot. Sauté in a pan with olive oil. Add the ground veal and brown for a few minutes.
Make Meat Sauce: Add the tomato sauce, reduce the heat, and simmer for about an hour. Season with salt and let it rest. Boil Pasta: Boil the pasta in salted water, draining it three to four minutes earlier than usual.
Mix and Transfer: Mix the pasta with some Parmesan, sauce half of the mozzarella, and transfer to a baking dish.
Top and Bake: Top with the remaining mozzarella, sauce, and Parmesan. Bake in the air fryer at 380°F for 15 minutes.
Serve: Let it cool slightly before serving.

MACARONI WITH BÉCHAMEL AND PECORINO

Servings: 2
Difficulty: Low
Cooking Time: 15 minutes

Ingredients:
- 1 1\3 cups of macaroni
- 2 cups of milk
- 7 oz pecorino cheese
- 2 Tbsp. of flour
- 3.5 oz diced cooked ham
- 1\4 cups of butter
- Pepper, to taste
- Salt, to taste
- Nutmeg, to taste

Instructions:
Prepare Béchamel Sauce: In a saucepan, melt the butter, add the flour and mix. Gradually add the milk, stirring continuously to avoid lumps. Cook on low heat until the sauce thickens. Season with salt, pepper, nutmeg, and most of the Pecorino (reserve some for topping).
Boil Macaroni: Boil the macaroni in salted water, draining it two minutes earlier than usual.
Mix and Transfer: Mix the macaroni with the diced ham and béchamel sauce. Transfer to a baking dish. Top and Bake: Sprinkle with the remaining Pecorino and bake in the air fryer at 380°F for 15 minutes.

PENNE WITH SPINACH SAUCE IN PARCHMENT

Servings: 2
Difficulty: Low
Cooking Time: 15 minutes

Ingredients:
- 1 1\3 cups of penne rigate
- 1.8 oz parmesan cheese
- 3\4 cups of spinach
- 1\8 cup of pine nuts
- 2 Tbsp. sliced almonds
- 1 oz pecorino cheese
- 1 sprig of marjoram
- 2 Tbsp of extra virgin olive oil
- 1 sprig of thyme
- 7 oz stracchino cheese
- 1 garlic clove
- Salt, to taste

Instructions:
Prepare Spinach Sauce: Wash and dry the spinach. Blend with garlic, thyme, marjoram, pine nuts, Pecorino, 1 oz of parmesan, and olive oil.
Boil Penne: Boil the penne in salted water, draining it two minutes earlier than usual. Mix with the spinach sauce and half of the stracchino cheese.
Assemble in Parchment: Place the pasta on parchment paper squares top with the remaining stracchino, Parmesan, and almond slices.
Seal and Bake: Seal the parchment packets and bake in the air fryer at 360°F for five minutes. Serve: Serve directly on the parchment.

TORTIGLIONI WITH MELTED CHEESE AND VEGETABLES

Servings: 4
Difficulty: Low
Cooking Time: 15 minutes

Ingredients:
- 1 cup of macaroni
- 1 mozzarella
- 3.5 oz smoked pancetta
- 2.8 oz grated parmesan cheese
- 2 zucchinis
- 2 Tbsp. of extra virgin olive oil
- 1 onion

Instructions:
Brown Pancetta: In a non-stick pan, brown the pancetta.
Sauté Onion and Zucchinis: Remove the pancetta and sauté the finely chopped onion in the rendered fat and olive oil. Add diced zucchini and sauté for a few minutes.
Boil Pasta: Boil the pasta in salted water, draining it a couple of minutes earlier than usual.
Mix Ingredients: Mix the pasta with the pancetta, zucchinis, 1.8 oz of parmesan, some cooking water, and diced mozzarella. Transfer and Bake: Transfer the mixture to a baking dish, sprinkle with the remaining parmesan, and bake at 370°F for 15 minutes.

CONCHIGLIONI WITH RICOTTA AND HAM

Servings: 4
Difficulty: Low
Cooking Time: 25 minutes

Ingredients:
- 1 cup of conchiglioni pasta
- 1.8 oz Pecorino Romano cheese
- 5.3 oz cooked ham
- 8.8 oz cow's milk ricotta
- 1 2\3 cups of béchamel sauce
- 7 oz mozzarella
- Salt, to taste
- Pepper, to taste

Instructions:
Cook Pasta: Cook the conchiglioni pasta until al dente.
Prepare Filling: In a bowl, combine: ricotta, salt, pepper, half of the grated cheese, ham, diced mozzarella, and some béchamel sauce. Prep Baking Dish: Spread a bit of béchamel sauce on the bottom of a baking dish.
Fill Conchiglioni: Fill the conchiglioni with the ricotta mixture and place them in the dish.
Top and Bake: Top with more béchamel and the remaining cheese. Bake in the air fryer at 370°F for 20 minutes.

TORTELLONI WITH BURRATA AND BASIL ON EGGPLANT CREAM

Servings: 2
Difficulty: Medium-High
Cooking Time: 15 minutes

Ingredients:
- 1 cup of semolina
- 2 eggs
- 1 burrata cheese
- 2 eggplants
- 1 oz pine nuts
- 1 garlic clove
- Some basil leaves
- 2 Tbsp. of extra virgin olive oil
- Salt

Instructions:
Prepare Burrata: Drain the burrata cheese in a colander.
Make Pasta Dough: In a bowl, mix semolina and eggs. Knead until smooth. Wrap it in plastic and let it rest.
Prepare Eggplants: Wash the eggplants. Grill one-half at 330°F for 20 minutes. Dice the other half and sauté in olive oil with garlic for 5 minutes. Season with salt.
Make Eggplant Sauce: Blend the grilled eggplant with garlic, salt, and olive oil to make a sauce.
Prepare Tortelloni: Roll out the pasta dough thinly. Cut into 2 in. squares and fill with diced eggplant. Fold into triangles and shape into tortelloni. Boil the tortelloni in salted water for five to six minutes.
Toast Pine Nuts: Toast the pine nuts in a pan.
Serve: Serve the tortelloni on a bed of eggplant sauce garnished with toasted pine nuts and basil leaves.

PUMPKIN LASAGNA

Servings: 4
Difficulty: Low
Cooking Time: 20 minutes

Ingredients:
- 2.8 oz parmesan cheese
- 7 oz smoked scamorza cheese
- 1 garlic clove
- 1 cup of broth
- fresh lasagna sheets
- 1 1\2 cups of pumpkin
- Extra virgin olive oil
- sprigs of rosemary
- Salt, to taste
- Pepper, to taste

For the Béchamel:
- 1 cup of milk
- 1\8 cup of butter
- 3 Tbsp. of flour
- Salt, to taste
- Pepper, to taste
- Nutmeg, to taste
-

Instructions:
Prepare Pumpkin: Clean the pumpkin, remove the skin, seeds, and fibers, and dice it.
Sauté Pumpkin: In a pan, sauté garlic and rosemary in olive oil. Add the pumpkin and cook for a few minutes. Add the broth and cook for 15 minutes. Season with salt and pepper. Let it cool, and remove the garlic.
Make Béchamel Sauce: Prepare the béchamel sauce.
Assemble Layers: In a baking dish that will fit into the air fryer, spread some béchamel, add a lasagna sheet, half of the pumpkin cubes, more béchamel, and grated cheese. Repeat layers.
Bake: Bake at 390°F for 20 minutes.

LASAGNA WITH GORGONZOLA AND WALNUTS

Servings: 4
Difficulty: Low
Cooking Time: 20 minutes

Ingredients:
- 4 fresh lasagna sheets
- 1\8 cup of butter
- 8.8 oz Gorgonzola cheese
- 1\8 cup of flour
- 3\4 cup of milk
- 3.5 oz grated parmesan cheese
- 1 cup of walnut kernels

Instructions:
Prepare Gorgonzola Sauce: In a saucepan, melt the butter, add flour, and gradually whisk in the milk until smooth. Add the Gorgonzola and whisk until melted. Stir in 0.9 oz of Parmesan.
Assemble Layers: In a baking dish, spread some Gorgonzola sauce, add a lasagna sheet, more sauce, Parmesan, and roughly chopped walnuts. Repeat layers.
Bake: Pour a bit of milk around the edges and bake at 390°F for 20 minutes. Rest Before Serving: Let it rest for ten minutes before serving.

MUSHROOM AND PUMPKIN LASAGNA

Servings: 4
Difficulty: Low
Cooking Time: 20 minutes

Ingredients:
- 4 fresh lasagna sheets
- Pepper, to taste
- 3\4 cup of champignon mushrooms
- Extra virgin olive oil
- 7 oz pumpkin
- 3.5 oz Parmesan cheese
- 1 small onion
- 1 cup of broth
- 5.3 oz smoked scamorza cheese
- 1 garlic clove
- A bunch of parsley
- Salt, to taste

Instructions:
Prepare Pumpkin and Mushrooms: Peel and dice the pumpkin. Clean and slice the mushrooms.
Sauté Pumpkin and Mushrooms: In a pan, heat some oil and sauté garlic. Add the pumpkin cubes and cook for a few minutes. Add the onion and sliced mushrooms. Cook for a few more minutes, then add the broth. Cook covered for ten minutes.
Season with salt, pepper, and finely chopped parsley.
Grate Scamorza Cheese: Grate the smoked scamorza cheese.
Layer Ingredients: In a baking dish, layer some of the mushroom and pumpkin mixture, a lasagna sheet, more of the mixture, scamorza cheese, and Parmesan. Repeat layers.
Bake: Bake in the air fryer at 390°F for 20 minutes. Check the doneness with a fork; it should be soft. Let it rest for a few minutes before serving.

BAKED NESTS

Servings: 2
Difficulty: Low
Cooking Time: 1 hour and 35 minutes

Ingredients:
- 1 cup of tagliatella nests
- 1 1\4 cups of béchamel sauce
- 1 1\4 cups of tomato sauce
- 8.8 oz ground beef
- 4\5 cup of water
- ½ onion
- 5.3 oz mozzarella
- 1 small carrot
- 5.3 oz scamorza cheese
- 1 small celery stalk
- 1.8 oz grated Parmesan cheese
- Extra virgin olive oil
- Salt, to taste

Instructions:
Prepare Vegetables: Wash and finely chop the celery, onion, and carrot.
Sauté Vegetables and Beef: In a pan with olive oil, sauté the vegetables. Add the ground beef and cook for a few minutes. Add the tomato sauce and simmer for ten minutes. Add water and continue cooking for 30 minutes. Season with salt and let it cool. Prepare Béchamel Sauce: Prepare the béchamel sauce and let it cool.
Assemble and Layer: In a baking dish, spread some meat sauce and place the tagliatella nests. Mix the béchamel with mozzarella, scamorza, and some meat sauce. Spoon this mixture over the nests. Cover with more meat sauce and sprinkle with Parmesan cheese. Bake: Bake at 370°F for 35 minutes.

BAKED WHEAT

Servings: 2
Difficulty: Low
Cooking Time: 35 minutes

Ingredients:
- 3\4 cup of wheat
- ½ onion
- 1 cup of water
- 3.5 oz grated Parmesan cheese
- 1 1\4 cups of tomato sauce
- Extra virgin olive oil
- Salt, to taste

Instructions:
Prepare Tomato Sauce: In a pan with olive oil, sauté the thinly sliced onion. Add the tomato sauce and simmer for ten minutes. Add water and continue cooking for 15 minutes.
Cook Wheat: Boil the wheat in salted water for 12 minutes and drain.
Mix and Assemble: Combine the cooked wheat with some tomato sauce and half of the parmesan cheese. In a baking dish, spread some sauce, add the wheat, and cover with the remaining sauce and parmesan. Bake: Bake in the air fryer at 390°F for 20 minutes.

MELTING WHEAT

Servings: 2
Difficulty: Low
Cooking Time: 35 minutes

Ingredients:
- 3\4 cup of wheat
- 3.5 oz grated parmesan cheese
- Extra virgin olive oil
- 1 1\4 cups of tomato sauce
- 3 Tbsp of breadcrumbs
- 1 cup of water
- 10.6 oz mozzarella
- ½ onion
- Salt, to taste

Instructions:
Prepare Wheat Mixture: Follow the same steps as the "Baked Wheat" recipe until the wheat is thoroughly mixed with tomato sauce and Parmesan.
Assemble and Layer: In a baking dish, spread some sauce, add half of the wheat, layer with mozzarella slices, and cover with the remaining wheat, additional sauce, breadcrumbs, and Parmesan. Bake: Bake in the air fryer at 390°F for 20 minutes.

WHEAT WITH CARDONCELLI MUSHROOMS AND CHERRY TOMATOES

Servings: 2
Difficulty: Low
Cooking Time: 40 minutes

Ingredients:
- 3\4 cups of wheat
- 3.5 oz grated parmesan cheese
- Extra virgin olive oil
- 1 1\4 cups of tomato sauce
- 3\4 cup of cardoncelli mushrooms
- 1 cup of water
- 1 garlic clove
- ½ onion
- 2\3 cup of cherry tomatoes
- Salt, to taste

Instructions:
Prepare Mushrooms and Tomatoes: Clean the mushrooms, slice them, and quarter the cherry tomatoes.
Sauté Mushrooms and Tomatoes: In a pan with olive oil, sauté the garlic. Add the mushrooms and cook for 15 minutes.
Incorporate the tomatoes and cook for a few more minutes. Season with salt and remove the garlic.
Prepare Tomato Sauce: In another pan, sauté the onion in olive oil. Add the tomato sauce, simmer for 10 minutes, add water, and continue cooking for 15 minutes.
Cook Wheat: Boil the wheat in salted water for 12 minutes and drain.
Mix and Assemble: Combine the cooked wheat with some tomato sauce, mushrooms, and half of the parmesan cheese. In a baking dish, spread some sauce, add the wheat mixture, and cover with the remaining sauce and parmesan. Bake: Bake in the air fryer at 390°F for 20 minutes.

BAKED PENNETTE WITH SPECK AND ZUCCHINI

Servings: 2
Difficulty: Low
Cooking Time: 20 minutes

Ingredients:
- 1 cup of pennette rigate
- 2 zucchinis
- Extra virgin olive oil
- 7 oz speck (smoked ham)
- 1 saffron sachet
- 3.5 oz grated parmesan cheese
- 1 garlic clove
- Salt, to taste

Instructions:
Boil the Pasta: Cook the Annette rigate in salted water and drain a few minutes before it's fully cooked. Prepare Zucchinis: Wash, trim, and slice the zucchinis.
Sauté Zucchinis and Speck: In a pan with olive oil, sauté the garlic. Add the sliced zucchini and cook for a few minutes. Then, add the speck slices. Dissolve saffron in a cup of pasta cooking water and add it to the pan. Simmer and season with salt.
Remove the garlic.
Mix Pasta with Sauce: Combine the pasta with some sauce and 2.8 oz of Parmesan cheese.
Assemble and Bake: In a baking dish, spread some sauce, add the pasta mixture, and cover with the remaining sauce and Parmesan. Bake in the air fryer at 380°F for 10 minutes.

BAKED FUSILLI WITH ASPARAGUS AND SPECK

Servings: 2
Difficulty: Low
Cooking Time: 20 minutes

Ingredients:
- 1 cup of fusilli
- 3.5 oz grated Parmesan cheese
- 1 cup of asparagus
- 7 oz speck (smoked ham)
- Extra virgin olive oil
- Salt, to taste

Instructions:
Boil the Pasta: Cook the fusilli in salted water and drain a few minutes before it's fully cooked.
Prepare Asparagus: Wash the asparagus, remove the woody ends, and cut the tips. Blanch the tips in boiling salted water for six minutes. In the last three minutes, add the sliced stems.
Sauté Asparagus and Speck: In a pan with olive oil, sauté garlic, then add the blanched asparagus and speck. Continue sautéing for a few more minutes.
Combine Ingredients: Add the partially cooked pasta, a cup of pasta cooking water, and most of the cheese to the pan. Mix well and transfer to a baking dish.
Sprinkle with Cheese and Bake: Sprinkle the remaining cheese on top and bake at 380°F for ten minutes.

STROZZAPRETI WITH SPECK AND WALNUTS

Servings: 2
Difficulty: Low
Cooking Time: 30 minutes

Ingredients:
- 1 cup of strozzapreti
- 3.5 oz smoked scamorza cheese
- 5.3 oz speck
- 1.8 oz grated parmesan cheese
- 1.8 oz walnut kernels
- 1 1\4 cups of béchamel sauce
- Salt, to taste

Instructions:
Boil the Pasta: Cook the strozzapreti in salted water until al dente.
Sauté the Speck: In a non-stick pan, sauté the speck.
Combine Ingredients: In a bowl, mix the cooked pasta, ⅔ of the béchamel sauce, chopped walnuts, smoked scamorza, and sautéed speck. Ensure thorough mixing.
Transfer to Baking Dish: Transfer the mixture to a baking dish.
Top and Bake: Top the mixture with the remaining béchamel and parmesan cheese. Bake in the air fryer at 360°F for 20 minutes.

LASAGNA WITH PORCINI MUSHROOMS

Servings: 2
Difficulty: Low
Cooking Time: 35 minutes

Ingredients:
- 5.3 oz fresh lasagna sheets
- 1.8 oz grated parmesan cheese
- 1 1\3 cups of champignon mushrooms
- Extra virgin olive oil
- 1\8 cup of dried porcini mushrooms
- 1 garlic clove
- 1\8 cup of truffle cream
- 1\4 cup of milk
- 1 1\4 cups of béchamel sauce

Instructions:
Soak the porcini mushrooms in warm water.
Clean and slice the champignon mushrooms.
In a pan with olive oil, sauté the garlic. Once hot, add the champignon and soaked porcini mushrooms. Cook for 5 minutes. Season with salt, remove the garlic and let it cool.
In a bowl, mix the béchamel sauce with the truffle cream and add the mushrooms. Mix well.
In a baking dish, spread some béchamel sauce diluted with milk. Layer the lasagna sheets and béchamel mixture, and continue until all ingredients are used.
Top with Parmesan cheese and bake at 370°F for 30 minutes. Let it cool before serving.

LASAGNA WITH ZUCCHINI, SHRIMP, AND PISTACHIO CRUMBLE

Servings: 2
Difficulty: Low
Cooking Time: 35 minutes

Ingredients:
- 4 fresh lasagna sheets
- 1\4 cup of pistachio crumble
- 2 zucchinis
- Extra virgin olive oil
- 10.6 oz shrimp
- 1 garlic clove
- 1 2\3 cup of béchamel sauce
- 1\4 cup of milk

Instructions:
Wash, trim, and slice the zucchini.
In a pan with olive oil, sauté the garlic. Once hot, add the zucchini and cook for five minutes. Add the shrimp and cook for a few more minutes. Remove the garlic and let it cool.
Prepare the béchamel sauce and dilute some of it with milk.
In a baking dish, spread some béchamel sauce. Layer the lasagna sheets, zucchini and shrimp mixture, and sprinkle some pistachio crumble. Continue layering until all ingredients are used.
Top with the remaining béchamel and pistachio crumble.
Bake in the air fryer at 370°F for 30 minutes. Let it cool before serving.

RIGATONI PIE

Servings: 2
Difficulty: Low
Cooking Time: 35 minutes

Ingredients:
- 3\4 cup of rigatoni
- 7 oz cow's ricotta
- Extra virgin olive oil
- 1 1\3 cups of spinach
- 1 garlic clove
- 1 1\4 cups of tomato sauce
- Salt, to taste

Instructions:
Prepare a simple tomato sauce.
In a pan with some olive oil, sauté the garlic. Add the spinach and cook. Remove the garlic and let it cool. Blend the spinach with the ricotta and transfer to a piping bag.
Boil the pasta in salted water until al dente.
Spread some tomato sauce at the bottom of a baking dish. Stand the rigatoni vertically, filling them with the ricotta and spinach mixture.
Top with more tomato sauce.
Bake at 360°F for 30 minutes. Let it cool before serving.

CAULIFLOWER GRATIN PIE

Servings: 2
Difficulty: Low
Cooking Time: 30 minutes

Ingredients:
- 3\4 cup of macaroni
- 3.5 oz smoked scamorza cheese
- 1 1\3 cups of cauliflower
- 1 garlic clove
- 3.5 oz grated parmesan cheese
- 1 chili pepper
- 1 1\4 cups of béchamel sauce
- Extra virgin olive oil
- Salt, to taste

Instructions:
Wash and slice the cauliflower.
Boil the pasta in salted water until al dente.
In a pan with some olive oil, sauté the garlic and chili pepper. Add the cauliflower and cook for 10-15 minutes, adding some pasta cooking water.
Add the pasta, ⅔ of the béchamel sauce, and half of the parmesan cheese. Mix well and transfer to a baking dish. Top with the remaining béchamel and Parmesan cheese. Bake in the air fryer at 370°F for 15 minutes.

MORTADELLA AND PROVOLONE PIE

Servings: 2
Difficulty: Low
Cooking Time: 40 minutes

Ingredients:
- 3\4 cup of penne rigate
- 5.3 oz provolone cheese
- 3.5 oz mortadella
- 3.5 oz grated parmesan cheese
- 1 cup of béchamel sauce

Instructions:
Boil the pasta in salted water and drain a few minutes before it's fully cooked. Transfer to a bowl and add ⅔ of the béchamel sauce and ⅔ of the Parmesan cheese, reserving some for later. Mix well.
In a baking dish, spread half of the pasta mixture. Layer with slices of mortadella and provolone. Add the remaining pasta and top with the reserved béchamel and parmesan cheese. Bake at 370°F for 30 minutes.

SEAFOOD CARTOCCI

Servings: 2
Difficulty: High
Cooking Time: 1 hour and 15 minutes

Ingredients:
- 3\4 cup of linguine
- 3.5 oz octopus
- A small bunch of parsley
- 3.5 oz cuttlefish
- 1\4 cup of butter
- 1 small leek
- 5.3 oz shrimp
- 1 small onion
- 2\3 cup of tomatoes
- 1\4 cup of white wine
- 1 garlic clove
- Extra virgin olive oil

Instructions:
Clean the shrimp by removing the head and shell.
Prepare the shrimp broth: Sauté leek and onion in a pot for a couple of minutes; add some parsley and the shrimp heads and shells. Cook for a few more minutes, deglaze with white wine, then cover with water and simmer for about an hour on low heat. Strain the broth.
Clean and cut the remaining seafood into small pieces. Wash and chop the tomatoes.
In a pan, heat olive oil and sauté garlic. Add seafood and tomatoes, and cook on low heat. Add a ladle of shrimp broth. Boil the linguine in salted water and drain. Add to the pan with seafood; mix in chopped parsley and butter.
Prepare two parchment paper sheets. Place one sheet in a baking dish, and add half of the pasta and some of its sauce. Seal the parchment paper and repeat with the other half.
Bake in the air fryer at 370°F for 15 minutes. Serve directly on the parchment paper, drizzled with olive oil and freshly ground pepper.

SALMON AND ROBIOLA PASTA BAKE

Servings: 2
Difficulty: Low
Cooking Time: 40 minutes

Ingredients:
- 3\4 cup of tortellini
- 1 cup of béchamel sauce
- 3.5 oz smoked salmon
- 5.3 oz robiola cheese

Instructions:
Boil the pasta in salted water and drain a few minutes before it's fully cooked.
Transfer to a bowl, and add ⅔ of the béchamel sauce, robiola, and finely chopped salmon. Mix well.
Transfer the mixture to a baking dish.
Top with the remaining béchamel sauce.
Bake in the air fryer at 370°F for 30 minutes.

BUCATINI PUTTANESCA

Servings: 2
Difficulty: Low
Cooking Time: 30 minutes

Ingredients:
- 7 oz bucatini
- 1 3\4 cups of canned peeled tomatoes
- A small bunch of parsley
- 3.5 oz black olives
- 1 chili pepper
- Oregano, to taste
- 1 garlic clove
- 2 Tbsp. of capers
- Extra virgin olive oil

Instructions:
In a pot, heat olive oil and sauté garlic and chopped chili pepper. Add tomatoes, crushing them with a fork, and cook for five minutes.
Add oregano, capers, and pitted olives. Season with salt.
Boil the bucatini in salted water until al dente, then add to the sauce.
Add chopped parsley, mix well, and transfer to a baking dish.
Drizzle with olive oil, sprinkle with more oregano, and bake in the air fryer at 360°F for 20 minutes.

PENNE WITH GUANCIALE AND WALNUTS

Servings: 2
Difficulty: Low
Cooking Time: 40 minutes

Ingredients:
- 2\3 cup of penne rigate
- 4.4 oz guanciale (pork cheek)
- Extra virgin olive oil
- 10 walnut kernels
- 1 onion
- 3.5 oz grated parmesan cheese
- 1 garlic clove
- 1\2 cup of cooking cream
- 1\3 cup of white wine
- 2 Tbsp. of tomato sauce
- Salt and pepper, to taste

Instructions:
Boil the penne in salted water until al dente.
Finely chop the garlic and onion and sauté in a pan with olive oil. Add guanciale cut into strips and chopped walnuts (reserving three for garnish).
Add the tomato sauce and cream. Season with salt and pepper. If needed, add some pasta cooking water to thin the sauce. Drain the pasta and add to the sauce. Mix well and transfer to a baking dish.
Sprinkle with cheese and the remaining chopped walnuts.
Bake in the air fryer at 370°F for 25 minutes.

OVEN-BAKED LASAGNA WITH CACIO E PEPE

Servings: 2
Difficulty: Low
Cooking Time: 20 minutes

Ingredients:
- 6 lasagna sheets
- 3.5 oz parmesan cheese
- 2 cups of béchamel sauce
- 5.3 oz mozzarella
- 3.5 oz pecorino cheese
- Salt, to taste
- Pepper, to taste

Instructions:
If using dried lasagna sheets, blanch them in boiling salted water to soften, then drain and cool on a clean cloth.
Slice the mozzarella and let it drain.
In a baking dish, spread some béchamel sauce. Layer with lasagna sheets, mozzarella, cheese, and a sprinkle of pepper.
Repeat layers until all ingredients are used.
Bake in the air fryer at 390°F for 20 minutes.

OVEN-BAKED PUMPKIN LASAGNA

Servings: 2
Difficulty: Medium
Cooking Time: 40 minutes

Ingredients:
- 6 lasagna sheets
- 1 1\2 cups of pumpkin
- 1 garlic clove 7 oz smoked scamorza cheese
- 1\4 cup of broth
- 1 sprig of rosemary
- 3.5 oz parmesan cheese
- Extra virgin olive oil
- Salt, to taste
- Pepper, to taste

Instructions:
If using dried lasagna sheets, blanch them in boiling salted water to soften, then drain and cool on a clean cloth.
Clean the pumpkin, removing skin, seeds, and fibers. Cut the flesh into cubes.
In a pan, heat olive oil and sauté garlic and rosemary. Add pumpkin and cook for a few minutes. Add broth and cook for 15 minutes with the lid on. Mash the pumpkin with a fork.
Layer the lasagna sheets in a baking dish with the pumpkin mixture.
Bake in the air fryer at 390°F for 20 minutes.

SECOND COURSES

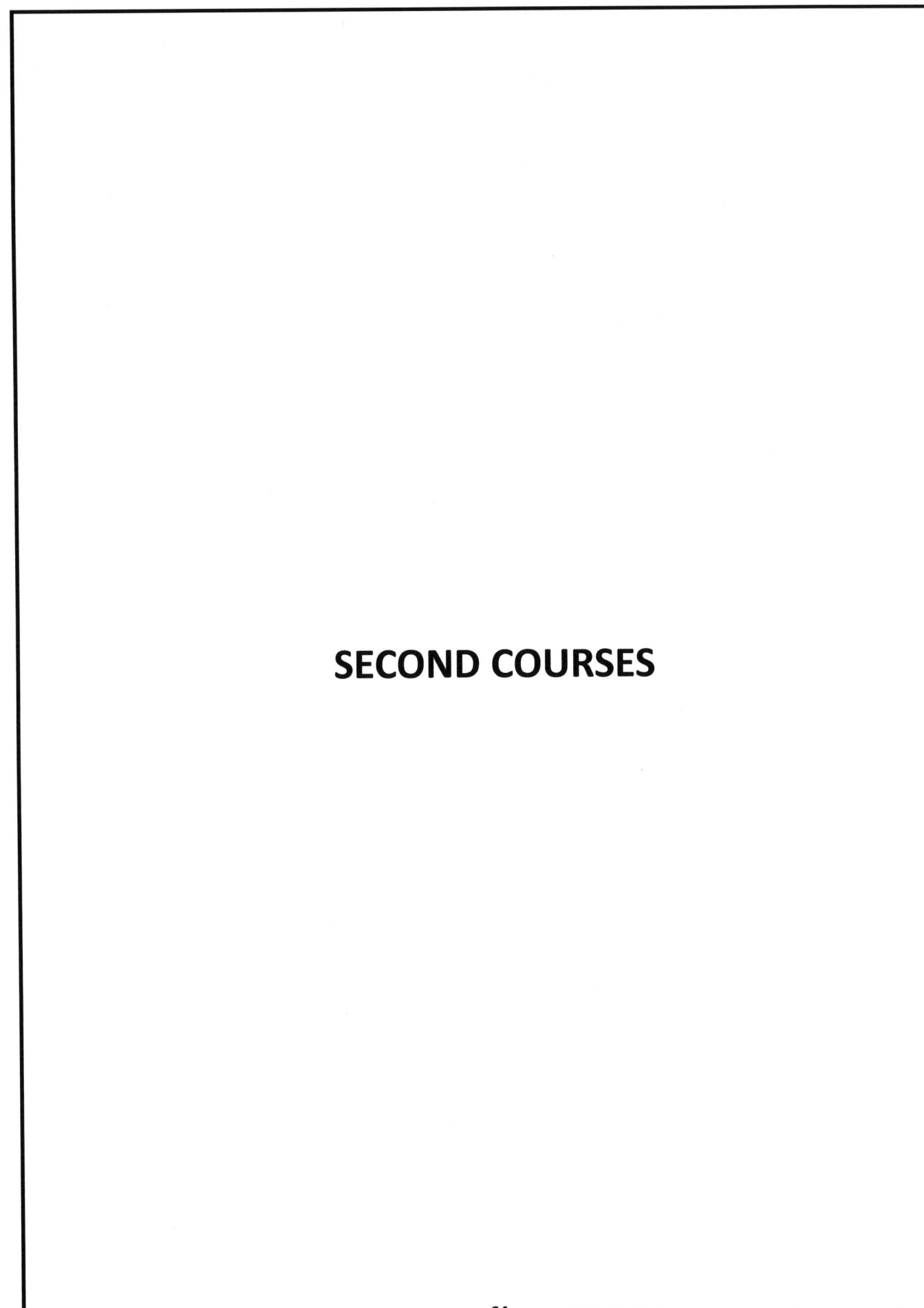

ROAST BEEF WITH VEGETABLE SAUCE

Servings: 4
Difficulty: High
Cooking Time: 55 minutes

Ingredients:
- 24.7 oz roast beef
- Rosemary
- Oil
- Salt to taste

Sauce:
- 1 carrot
- 1 celery stalk
- 1 onion
- 1 small potato
- Extra virgin olive oil

Instructions:
Tie the roast beef, incorporating rosemary sprigs with the twine. Sear the meat in a large pan with some oil, add roughly chopped vegetables, and continue searing until all sides of the meat are browned. This will keep the meat juicy inside. Transfer everything to the fryer basket and cook at 370°F for 45 minutes, turning halfway through.
After cooking, let the meat rest. Blend the vegetables with their juices, seasoning with salt and adding water if needed. Slice the roast beef and serve with the sauce.

SESAME BREADED CHICKEN

Servings: 2
Difficulty: Low
Cooking Time: 10 minutes

Ingredients:
- 4 chicken breast slices
- Paprika
- Garlic powder
- 2 Tbsp. of sesame seeds
- Bread crumbs to taste
- Salt to taste
- Oil to taste

Instructions:
In a bowl, combine bread crumbs, salt, paprika, garlic powder, and sesame seeds.
Coat the chicken slices with the breadcrumb mixture.
Place the chicken on perforated parchment paper on the grill.
Cook in the air fryer at 360°F for 10 minutes, turning halfway through.

CHICKEN BUNDLES WITH SPECK AND SCAMORZA

Servings: 4
Difficulty: Low
Cooking Time: 15 minutes

Ingredients:
- 8 thin chicken breast slices
- 4 slices of scamorza cheese (or Emmental or other cheese of choice)
- 2 eggs
- 4 slices of speck
- 1 Tbsp. of grated cheese Salt
- Bread crumbs to taste
- Flour to taste

Instructions:
Use a meat mallet or glass to flatten the chicken slices. Fold the cheese slice in half, wrap it with speck, and place it on one end of the chicken slice. Roll the chicken around the filling. Dredge the rolls in flour, then egg, and finally in bread crumbs mixed with grated cheese and salt. Ensure the ends are sealed to prevent cheese from leaking out.
Place on the air fryer grill with perforated parchment paper and bake at 370°F for 15 minutes, turning halfway through.

HAMBURGER

Servings: 2
Difficulty: Medium
Cooking Time: 15 minutes

Ingredients:
- 10.6 oz veal mince
- ½ golden onion
- 2 Tbsp. of bread crumbs
- 2 Tbsp. of grated cheese
- Salt
- Pepper

Instructions:
In a bowl, combine the minced meat, cheese, bread crumbs, salt, pepper, and finely chopped onion.
Form the hamburgers and let them rest in the fridge for 30 minutes.
Cook the hamburgers at 360°F for 15 minutes in the air fryer grill without parchment paper, allowing the fat to drip into the basket. Turn halfway through. Serve the hamburgers with lettuce leaves and mayonnaise.

CHICKEN WINGS WITH POTATOES IN SAUCE

Servings: 2
Difficulty: Low
Cooking Time: 30 minutes

Ingredients:
- 6 chicken wings
- 3-4 potatoes
- ½ glass of white wine
- ½ onion Salt
- Olive oil
- Rosemary

Instructions:
Wash and peel the potatoes, cut them into cubes, and soak them in cold water for about 30 minutes.
Drain the potatoes and place them in a baking dish, adding sliced onion, chicken wings, salt, olive oil, white wine, and a sprig of rosemary. Mix everything well.
Place the dish in the fryer basket and set it to 370°F for about 30 minutes, stirring occasionally. Check the potatoes' doneness with a fork; they should be easily pierced.

STUFFED BELL PEPPERS WITH MEAT

Servings: 2
Difficulty: Low
Cooking Time: 30 minutes

Ingredients:
- 1 yellow bell pepper
- 3 Tbsp. of bread crumbs
- 2.1 oz grated cheese
- 1 red bell pepper
- 1 egg
- 8.8 oz minced meat
- Salt to taste
- Pepper to taste

Instructions:
Wash and dry the bell peppers, remove the stem and seeds, and cut each pepper into four pieces. Place them in a baking dish with a drizzle of olive oil.
In a bowl, mix the minced meat, cheese, bread crumbs, egg, salt, and pepper. Use this mixture to stuff the bell pepper pieces. Bake in the air fryer at 360°F for about 30 minutes.

BELL PEPPER BOATS WITH TUNA

Servings: 2
Difficulty: Low
Cooking Time: 25-30 minutes

Ingredients:
- 2 bell peppers (yellow and red)
- 2 cans of drained tuna
- 2 Tbsp. of grated cheese
- 2 Tbsp. of bread crumbs
- Pitted black olives
- Pepper to taste
- Extra virgin olive oil
- Capers
- Salt to taste

Instructions:
Wash and dry the bell peppers, remove the stem and seeds, and cut each pepper into four pieces. Place them in a baking dish with a drizzle of olive oil.
Season the bell pepper boats with salt and pepper. In each cavity, add some tuna, five to six capers, some cheese, and bread crumbs. Top with sliced olives.
Bake in the air fryer at 360°F for 25-30 minutes.

STUFFED POTATOES WITH TUNA

Servings: 4
Difficulty: Medium-Low
Cooking Time: 22 minutes

Ingredients:
- 4 potatoes
- 2.1 oz grated cheese
- 5.3 oz drained tuna
- 1\3 cup of pitted olives
- 1 Tbsp. of capers
- Parsley
- Pepper
- Salt

Instructions:
Wash the potatoes and boil them for about 10 minutes. Check for doneness with a fork; they should be soft but not falling apart. Drain and let them cool.
Peel the potatoes and cut them in half. Scoop out some of the insides to form boats. Place them in a baking dish with a drizzle of olive oil. In a bowl, mash the scooped-out potato and add finely chopped parsley, tuna, olives, capers, and cheese. Mix well. Use this mixture to stuff the potato boats.
Bake in the air fryer at 370°F for 10-12 minutes.
Tip: The potato boats can be filled in various ways, such as with speck and smoked scamorza, ham, gorgonzola and chopped walnuts, mortadella and pistachio crumbs, or any other combination you can imagine. They are great for parties when presented on a tray with various fillings and can be served in paper cups for appetizers.

CHICKEN BRACIOLETTE

Servings: 2
Difficulty: Medium-Low
Cooking Time: 40 minutes

Ingredients:
- 4 chicken thighs
- 4 slices of smoked scamorza cheese
- 4 slices of speck
- Kitchen twine

Instructions:
Have the butcher debone the chicken thighs for you.
Lay them out on a cutting board and flatten them slightly with a meat mallet or the bottom of a glass.
Place a slice of speck and a slice of scamorza cheese on each chicken thigh. Roll them up and secure them with kitchen twine to ensure they don't open during cooking.
Place them on the air fryer grill and cook at 370°F for 25-30 minutes, turning halfway. Then, increase the temperature to 380°F for another 10 minutes.

PORK TENDERLOIN IN CRUST

Servings: 4
Difficulty: Medium-Low
Cooking Time: 35 minutes

Ingredients:
- 4 pork or beef tenderloin slices (about 0.4 inch thick)
- 1 rectangular puff pastry roll (1\2 inch thick)
- 1 1\3 cups of mixed mushrooms (champignon, cardoncelli, and porcini)
- Extra virgin olive oil
- 4 slices of Galbanino cheese
- 1 garlic clove
- 3.5 oz speck

Instructions:
Rub the tenderloin slices with a bit of oil on all sides and grill them in the air fryer for five minutes at 390°F to seal them, keeping them tender and juicy inside.
Meanwhile, clean and slice the mushrooms. Sauté them in a pan with garlic and julienned speck for about 10 minutes. Take the puff pastry out of the fridge, unroll it, and divide it into four. Place a slice of the cooled tenderloin in the center of each rectangle, add a generous spoonful of mushrooms, and cover with a slice of cheese. Seal the edges well, moistening them slightly with water.
Place them on the air fryer grill with the sealed side down on perforated parchment paper. Cook at 390°F for 15 minutes, turn, and continue cooking for another 15 minutes.
Tip: Remove the puff pastry from the fridge about 10 minutes before using it to prevent it from breaking when unrolling.

PAPRIKA CHICKEN THIGHS

Servings: 4
Difficulty: Low
Cooking Time: 15 minutes

Ingredients:
- 8 chicken thighs
- Garlic powder
- 1 sprig of rosemary
- Oil to taste
- Paprika
- Salt

Instructions:
In a bowl, place the chicken thighs, drizzle or brush with oil.
Add rosemary, garlic, and paprika powder. Mix well to coat all sides of the chicken.
Cook at 390°F for about 15 minutes, turning occasionally for even browning. Depending on your preference, you can use sweet or spicy paprika or even barbecue sauce.

MEATBALLS

Servings: 4
Difficulty: Medium-Low
Cooking Time: 20 minutes

Ingredients:
- 10.6 oz ground beef
- 1 egg
- 1.8 oz grated Parmesan cheese
- 1 garlic clove or garlic powder
- 2 Tbsp. of bread crumbs
- Parsley
- Salt
- Pepper

Instructions:
In a bowl, combine ground beef, bread crumbs, grated Parmesan, garlic, finely chopped parsley, egg, salt, and pepper. Mix well.
Using a spoon, form meatballs and place them on the air fryer grill covered with perforated parchment paper. Cook at 360°F for 20 minutes, shaking halfway through to ensure even cooking.

MARINATED CHICKEN THIGHS WITH YOGURT

Servings: 4
Difficulty: Low
Cooking Time: 30 minutes

Ingredients:
- 8 chicken thighs
- 1 glass of white wine or lemon juice
- 2 Tbsp. of paprika
- ½ glass of olive oil
- 1 pot of plain yogurt Parsley
- 1 Tbsp. honey
- Thyme
- Garlic
- Rosemary
- Pepper
- Salt

Instructions:
Finely chop the herbs and garlic and place them in a glass container.
Add wine or lemon juice, salt, pepper, oil, paprika (sweet or spicy, depending on your preference), honey, and yogurt. Whisk vigorously to create an emulsion.
Add the chicken thighs, cover the container with plastic wrap or a lid, and marinate in the fridge for at least two to three hours. After marinating, place the chicken on the air fryer grill. Cook at 390°F for 30 minutes, shaking occasionally to ensure even cooking of the meat.
The marinade helps to eliminate the typical smell of chicken and keeps it moist and juicy.

SALMON FILLET WITH PISTACHIO CRUST

Servings: 2
Difficulty: Medium
Cooking Time: 15 minutes

Ingredients:
- 2 salmon fillets, each 7 oz
- 2 Tbsp. of breadcrumbs
- 1\4 cup of unsalted pistachios
- A small bunch of parsley

Instructions:
In a mixer, combine pistachios, parsley, and breadcrumbs. Blend until finely chopped.
Transfer the mixture to a plate and coat the skinned salmon fillets on both sides.
Place them on perforated parchment paper and cook in the air fryer at 370°F for 15 minutes.

COD FILLET MARINATED IN YOGURT AND BREADED

Servings: 2
Difficulty: Medium-Low
Cooking Time: 15 minutes

Ingredients:
- 14 oz cod fillet
- 3\4 cup of plain yogurt
- Pepper to taste
- 2-3 small bunches of parsley
- A few chives
- 1\4 cup of crackers
- Olive oil to taste
- Salt to taste

Instructions:
In a mixer, finely chop parsley and chives. Mix them with yogurt and season with salt and pepper.
Pour the yogurt mixture into a container, coat the fillets on both sides and let them marinate in the refrigerator for about an hour, covered with plastic wrap or a lid.
After marinating, finely crumble the crackers in a mixer and bread the fillets on both sides.
Preheat the air fryer to 390°F for three minutes, place the fillets on the grill, and cook at 370°F for about 15 minutes.

SAVORY BASKETS FILLED WITH SHRIMP

Servings: 6
Difficulty: Medium
Cooking Time: 6 minutes

Ingredients:
- 1 1\3 cups of all-purpose flour
- 2\3 cup of frozen butter, cubed
- 1\4 cup of cold water
- 1 tsp. salt

Filling:
- 7 oz shrimp
- Cocktail sauce
- 2 lettuce leaves

Instructions:
In a bowl, combine flour, salt, cubed butter, and cold water. Quickly crumble the mixture with your hands. Let the dough rest for 30 minutes, wrapped in plastic wrap.
Roll out the dough between two sheets of parchment paper and cut out discs using a round cookie cutter or glass.
Place the discs on inverted muffin tins on the grill and cook in the air fryer at 360°F for six minutes.
Fill them only a few minutes before serving to prevent the baskets from getting too soft due to the moisture of the filling.

SAVORY BASKETS FILLED WITH BRESAOLA AND AVOCADO

Servings: 6
Difficulty: Medium
Cooking Time: 6 minutes

Ingredients:
- 10.6 oz all-purpose flour
- 2\3 cup of frozen butter, cubed
- 1 tsp. of salt
- 1\4 cup of cold water

Filling:
- 3.5 oz bresaola
- 1 lemon
- ½ avocado
- 1 oz Grana cheese flakes
- A small bunch of arugula
- Olive oil to taste
- Pepper to taste
- Salt to taste

Instructions:
In a bowl, combine flour, salt, cubed butter, and cold water. Quickly crumble the mixture with your hands. Let the dough rest in the refrigerator for 30 minutes, wrapped in plastic wrap.
Meanwhile, slice the avocado. On a plate, lay out the bresaola slices. On each slice, add torn arugula, Grana cheese flakes, and avocado. Season with salt and pepper. In a small bowl, prepare a citronette using freshly squeezed lemon juice (strained to remove seeds and pulp) and a bit of olive oil. Whisk vigorously with a fork and set aside.
Roll out the dough between two sheets of parchment paper and cut out discs using a cookie cutter.
Place the discs on inverted muffin tins on the grill and cook in the air fryer at 360°F for six minutes.
Once cooled, fill each basket with two slices of bresaola, including arugula and avocado. Once all baskets are filled, drizzle with the citronette.

TOMINI WITH MORTADELLA AND PISTACHIO CRUST

Servings: 4
Difficulty: Low
Cooking Time: 10 minutes

Ingredients:
- 4 Tominis (small soft cheese)
- 2 slices of mortadella
- 4 Tbsp. of pistachio crumbs

Instructions:
Place the Tominis on a sheet of parchment paper and make incisions on the top. Bake at 360°F for ten minutes. Once cooked, place them on a serving dish and decorate with mortadella and pistachio crumbs.

PUFF PASTRY WITH CABBAGE, SAUSAGE, AND CHEESE

Servings: 4
Difficulty: Medium-High
Cooking Time: 45 minutes

Ingredients:
- 2 round puff pastry packages
- 3.5 oz cheddar cheese
- 1 cup of black cabbage
- 1.8 oz grated Parmesan cheese
- 7 oz sausage
- 1 egg yolk + 1 tsp. of milk
- 5.3 oz smoked scamorza cheese
- Sesame and poppy seeds to taste

Instructions:
Remove the puff pastries from the refrigerator and set them aside. Peel the sausage, crumble it, and place it in an air fryer basket with a garlic clove. Cook at 370°F for seven minutes, stirring often for even cooking.
Wash the black cabbage, remove the hard parts, chop it, and add it to the sausage. Continue cooking for another eight minutes at 340°F, stirring halfway through.
Grate the scamorza and cheddar cheese and mix them with the Parmesan.
Unroll one puff pastry and, with its paper, line a baking dish (I use a 7.9-inch diameter dish). Spread it out well, avoiding folds, and prick it with a fork.
Add the grated cheese to the sausage and cabbage mixture, mix well, and pour into the puff pastry. Cover with the second puff pastry and seal the edges well to prevent the cheese from leaking out. Beat the egg yolk with milk, brush the surface, and sprinkle with sesame and poppy seeds.
Bake at 370°F for 30 minutes.

GRATINATED SWORDFISH

Servings: 4
Difficulty: Medium-High
Cooking Time: 10 minutes

Ingredients:
- 4 swordfish fillets
- 1 Tbsp. of grated cheese
- 1\4 cup of breadcrumbs
- 2 small bunches of parsley
- 5 cherry tomatoes
- Garlic
- Thyme
- Pepper to taste
- Salt to taste

Instructions:
Place the swordfish on a baking tray lined with parchment paper.
Finely chop the herbs and garlic. Quarter the cherry tomatoes and combine them in a bowl with the grated cheese, breadcrumbs, a pinch of salt, a grind of pepper, and a drizzle of olive oil.
Sprinkle the mixture over the swordfish fillets, drizzle with olive oil, and bake at 360°F for ten minutes.

SALMON FILLET IN PARCHMENT

Servings: 2
Difficulty: Low
Cooking Time: 15 minutes

Ingredients:
- 10.6 oz salmon fillet (2 fillets)
- Olive oil to taste
- 1 lemon
- A bunch of arugula
- ½ avocado
- Pepper to taste
- Salt to taste

Instructions:
Grate some lemon zest and set aside. Slice a few pieces of the lemon and squeeze the rest.
Cut the salmon into two fillets. Drizzle olive oil over the salmon fillets on all sides and place them on a sheet of parchment paper. Drizzle with lemon juice and cover the fillets with lemon slices. Wrap the parchment paper tightly to prevent any liquid from escaping and to keep the salmon moist. Bake at 360°F for 15 minutes.
Meanwhile, wash the arugula and slice the avocado. Prepare a bed of arugula and avocado on a plate, place the salmon in the center, and season with salt, freshly ground pepper, lemon juice, and grated lemon zest.

MEAT AND SPINACH FRITTATA

Servings: 2
Difficulty: Low
Cooking Time: 43 minutes

Ingredients:
- 1 1\3 cups of spinach
- 1\4 cup of breadcrumbs
- 5.3 oz ground veal and pork mix
- 5.3 oz mozzarella
- 2 eggs
- 1 garlic clove
- 2.8 oz Parmesan cheese
- Olive oil to taste
- Milk to taste
- Salt to taste
- Pepper to taste

Instructions:
In a pan, sauté the ground meat with a bit of garlic.
Wash the spinach well. If using fresh spinach, tear the leaves directly into a bowl. If using frozen spinach, cook at 340°F for about 12-13 minutes in the air fryer.
Add breadcrumbs, cooled ground meat, eggs, cheese, salt, and pepper, and diced mozzarella to the spinach. Mix everything together and add a bit of milk to make the mixture soft.
Pour the mixture into a baking dish and bake at 370°F for 25-30 minutes.

MUSHROOMS STUFFED WITH BREAD

Servings: 2
Difficulty: Low
Cooking Time: 20 minutes

Ingredients:
- 10 mushrooms
- 3 slices of white bread
- ½ cup of milk
- 1 bunch of parsley
- 1.8 oz grated cheese
- 1 garlic clove
- ½ cup of vegetable broth
- Olive oil to taste
- Pepper to taste
- Salt to taste

Instructions:
Clean the mushrooms of any dirt, rinse them quickly, and dry them.
Gently detach the mushroom stems and scrape a bit of the inside to make room for the filling. Chop the stems. In a pan with a bit of olive oil and garlic, sauté the chopped mushroom stems for four to five minutes.
Soak the bread in a bowl with milk.
Squeeze out the bread and add it to the chopped parsley, break the eggs, add the cheese, salt, and pepper, and mix everything together.
Fill the mushroom caps with the mixture and sprinkle with some Parmesan.
Add the broth to the baking dish among the mushrooms and bake at 360°F for 10-15 minutes.

TUNA STUFFED EGGS

Servings: 2
Difficulty: Low
Cooking Time: 15 minutes

Ingredients:
- 4 eggs
- 1 Tbsp. of capers
- 1 can of tuna
- Generous Tbsp. of mayonnaise

Instructions:
Place the eggs in the air fryer basket and set it to 270°F for 15 minutes.
Prepare a bowl with cold water and place the eggs in it after cooking to cool them down.
Peel the eggs and cut them in half lengthwise. With a spoon, remove the yolks, crumble them with a fork, add chopped capers (saving some for decoration), tuna and mayonnaise, and mix everything together. Fill the egg whites with the mixture and garnish with a whole caper.

ZUCCHINI AND SAUSAGE SKEWERS

Servings: 2
Difficulty: Low
Cooking Time: 15 minutes

Ingredients:
- 1 zucchini
- 7-8 sausage pieces
- 1 Tbsp. of breadcrumbs
- 1 Tbsp. of grated cheese
- Olive oil
- Pepper to taste
- Salt to taste

Instructions:
Wash, dry, and trim the zucchini, and slice it lengthwise.
Drizzle the zucchini slices with olive oil and place them on the air fryer grill, setting it to 360°F for five minutes. Continue this process until all zucchini slices are cooked.
Season the zucchini slices with salt and pepper in a bowl. Cut the sausage pieces into four parts each.
Take a zucchini slice and wrap it around a piece of sausage. Continue this process until all the zucchini slices and sausage pieces are used.
Thread about five wrapped pieces onto each skewer, coat them in breadcrumbs and cheese, and cook at 390°F for about ten minutes, turning halfway through.

STUFFED MUSHROOMS WITH MEAT

Servings: 2
Difficulty: Low
Cooking Time: 20 minutes

Ingredients:
- 10 mushrooms
- 2 eggs
- 1 bunch of parsley
- 1 garlic clove
- 1.8 oz grated cheese
- Half cup of ground beef
- ½ cup of vegetable broth
- Olive oil to taste
- Pepper to taste
- Salt to taste

Instructions:
Clean the mushrooms, rinse them quickly, and dry them.
Gently detach the mushroom stems, scrape a bit of the inside to make room for the filling, and chop them. In a pan with some olive oil and garlic, sauté the chopped mushroom stems for four to five minutes.
In a bowl, combine the ground meat, chopped parsley, eggs, cheese, salt, and pepper. Mix well.
Fill the mushroom caps with the mixture, place them in a baking dish with the filling facing up, and sprinkle with some cheese. Add the broth to the baking dish among the mushrooms and bake at 360°F for 15-20 minutes.

MARINATED CHICKEN BREAST WITH AVOCADO AND LAMB'S LETTUCE

Servings: 4
Difficulty: Medium
Cooking Time: 20-25 minutes

Ingredients:
- 21 oz chicken breast
- Garlic
- 2 lemons + ½ for salad dressing
- Lamb's lettuce (Valerian)
- ½ cup of olive oil
- ½ avocado
- 2 sprigs of rosemary
- Olive oil for dressing the lamb's lettuce
- Paprika
- Salt to taste

Instructions:
For the marinade, squeeze the lemon juice and whisk in the olive oil to create an emulsion. Add the chopped rosemary sprigs, paprika, and chopped garlic. Immerse the chicken (cut in half and bone removed) in the marinade. Cover with plastic wrap and let it rest for at least 30 minutes.
Preheat the air fryer to 390°F for three minutes.
Wrap the chicken in parchment paper, ensuring the closure is at the bottom. Place it on the grill and set the air fryer to 390°F for 20-25 minutes.
Wash the lamb's lettuce and slice the avocado. Slice the chicken into strips and place it on a bed of salad. Season with salt, olive oil, and lemon juice.

SWORDFISH MEATBALLS

Servings: 4
Difficulty: Medium
Cooking Time: 20 minutes

Ingredients:
- 1 potato
- 10.6 oz swordfish
- 1 sprig of thyme
- 1 egg
- Milk to taste
- 1.4 oz grated parmesan cheese
- Breadcrumbs to taste
- Pepper to taste
- Salt to taste

Instructions:
Boil the potato.
In a mixer, combine the fish pulp, boiled potato, egg, grated Parmesan, salt, and pepper. Blend until well combined. Gradually add milk and breadcrumbs until you achieve a smooth, compact, and workable mixture.
Form into meatballs, spray them with oil, place them in the air fryer basket, and cook at 390°F for 20 minutes.

POUCHES OF SCAMORZA CHEESE WITH SPECK AND WALNUTS

Servings: 4
Difficulty: Medium
Cooking Time: 8 minutes

Ingredients:
- 4 slices of Scamorza cheese, 1\4 in. thick
- 12 slices of speck (smoked ham)
- 10 walnut kernels
- Milk to taste

Instructions:
Coarsely chop the walnuts.
Dip the Scamorza cheese slices in milk and coat them on all sides with the walnuts. Wrap them in Speck, ensuring the cheese is fully covered to prevent it from leaking out. Place them on a tray and set the air fryer to 370°F for eight minutes.

BREAD BOWLS WITH SPICY MARINATED SHRIMP IN MANGO SAUCE

Servings: 4
Difficulty: Medium
Cooking Time: 17 minutes

Ingredients:
- 14 oz shrimp
- 1 lemon
- 1 garlic clove
- 1 chili pepper
- 4 slices of white bread
- Olive oil to taste
- Flour to taste
- Salt to taste

For the mango sauce:
- ½ cup of mango
- ½ lemon
- 1 tsp. honey
- 1 Tbsp. of mustard
- 1 Tbsp. of olive oil

Instructions:
Clean the shrimp, rinse them, and let them drain in a colander. Cut the shrimp into rings, transfer them to a paper towel to dry, and then place them in a freezer bag with flour. Shake well to coat the shrimp in flour.
For the marinade, combine lemon juice, olive oil, crushed garlic clove, salt, and chopped chili pepper in a bowl. Add the shrimp and let them marinate.
Preheat the air fryer to 390°F for three minutes. Place the shrimp in the basket and cook for 13 minutes, shaking occasionally for even browning.
For the mango sauce, blend the mango pulp, mustard, honey, lemon, salt, and olive oil until smooth.
Flatten the bread slices with a rolling pin, spray them with oil, season with salt, pepper, and garlic powder on both sides and place them on overturned muffin tins. Bake at 370°F for four minutes. Fill the bread bowls with marinated shrimp and top with mango sauce.

FRIED CALAMARI

Servings: 4
Difficulty: Medium
Cooking Time: 9 minutes

Ingredients:
- 10.6 oz calamari
- Extra virgin olive oil spray
- Flour to taste
- Salt, to taste

Instructions:
Clean the calamari thoroughly, rinse them, and let them drain in a colander.
Cut the calamari into rings and place them on a paper towel to dry.
Transfer the calamari to a freezer bag, add flour, seal the bag, and shake well to coat the calamari in flour. Preheat the air fryer to 390°F for three minutes.
Spray some oil in the basket, place the calamari rings in the basket, ensuring they are spaced out, spray them with a couple more puffs of oil, and cook at 390°F for nine minutes, shaking occasionally for even browning.
Once done, transfer them to a serving plate and season with a light sprinkle of salt.

BREADED PORK STEAKS

Servings: 2
Difficulty: Medium-Low
Cooking Time: 15 minutes

Ingredients:
- 2 pork steaks
- 1 egg
- Breadcrumbs to taste
- 1 sprig of rosemary
- 1 Tbsp. of grated cheese
- 1 garlic clove
- 1 Tbsp. of paprika
- Extra virgin olive oil
- 1 tsp. of garlic powder
- Flour to taste

Instructions:
Massage the steak with a spray of oil on both sides.
Prepare three plates for breading: the first with flour, the second with the beaten egg, and the third with breadcrumbs, cheese, paprika, and garlic powder.
Coat the steaks first in flour, then in egg, and finally in the flavored breadcrumbs. Place them on the grill, spray them with a bit of oil to facilitate browning, set them to 370°F, and cook for about 15 minutes. The cooking time may vary based on the thickness of the meat.

MEATBALLS IN BACON

Servings: 4
Difficulty: Medium-Low
Cooking Time: 20 minutes

Ingredients:
- 12 slices of bacon
- 1 egg
- 10.6 oz ground beef
- 1\4 cup of breadcrumbs
- 1\4 cup of grated parmesan cheese
- 2 sprigs of rosemary
- Pepper to taste
- Salt to taste

Instructions:
In a bowl, combine the ground beef, cheese, egg, breadcrumbs, salt, and pepper. Mix well and form into small cylinders. Wrap each meat cylinder with a slice of bacon and place them in a baking dish. Add the rosemary sprigs and set the air fryer to 360°F for 20 minutes, turning halfway through.

TURKEY ROLL WITH VEGETABLES

Servings: 4
Difficulty: Medium
Cooking Time: 20 minutes

Ingredients:
- 21 oz turkey breast
- 1 small bunch of marjoram
- ½ yellow bell pepper
- 1 tsp. of sugar
- ½ red bell pepper
- 3 basil leaves
- ½ eggplant
- 1 garlic clove
- 1 carrot
- 1 cup of white wine
- 1 celery stalk
- 1 tbsp. of capers
- 6 black olives
- 2 Tbsp. of white wine vinegar
- Extra virgin olive oil
- Tbsp. of tomato puree
- Salt to taste
- Pepper to taste

Instructions:
Dice the bell peppers, eggplant, carrot, and celery, keeping them separate.
In a pot with a bit of oil and garlic, sauté the carrot and celery for three minutes. Add the bell peppers, and after another two minutes, add the eggplant. Cook for five minutes on medium heat, then add the tomato puree, olive slices, and capers. Deglaze with white wine and cook for another five minutes. If needed, add half a cup of water and cook until the vegetables soften when pressed with a fork.
Add the vinegar and sugar, mix well, and turn off the heat. Season with salt, add a pinch of pepper, and the basil leaves. Let it cool, and remove the garlic. Lay out the turkey slices on a cutting board, overlapping them slightly. Flatten them with a meat mallet. Cover with the vegetable mixture. Roll up the meat and secure it with cooking twine.
Place the roll in a baking dish, spray with a bit of oil, add the marjoram, and roast in a preheated oven for ten minutes, turning frequently to seal all sides. Add half a cup of wine and continue cooking at 360°F for 35 minutes. Let it cool before slicing to prevent it from falling apart. Skewer the slices for appetizers and cut them into 0.6-inch thick slices. Serve on a bed of lamb's lettuce or lettuce leaves.

CHICKEN DRUMSTICKS WITH TZATZIKI SAUCE

Servings: 2
Difficulty: Medium-Low
Cooking Time: 25 minutes

Ingredients:
- 6 chicken drumsticks
- Breadcrumbs
- 1 tsp. of paprika
- 1 sprig of rosemary
- Extra virgin olive oil
- Salt to taste

Tzatziki:
- 7 oz Greek yogurt
- 1 garlic clove
- 1 Tbsp. of white wine vinegar
- 1 cucumber
- 1 Tbsp. of olive oil
- Fine salt to taste

Instructions:

For the Tzatziki:
Wash the cucumber and grate it with the skin on. Place it in a colander over a bowl and let it drain for at least an hour. Peel the garlic cloves, remove the germ, and crush them into a paste.
In a bowl, combine the yogurt, salt, oil, and vinegar. Squeeze out any excess water from the cucumber and add it to the yogurt. Add the garlic paste and mix well. Refrigerate for two to three hours.

For the Chicken Drumsticks:
In a small bowl, combine the breadcrumbs, salt, paprika, and chopped rosemary needles.
Spray the chicken drumsticks with a little oil and coat them in the flavored breadcrumbs.
Preheat the air fryer to 390°F for three minutes and cook at 390°F for 15 minutes. Then, reduce the temperature to 340°F and cook for another ten minutes.
Serve the drumsticks with the Tzatziki sauce.

GRATINATED SCALLOPS

Servings: 4
Difficulty: Low
Cooking Time: 7 minutes

Ingredients:
- 8 scallops
- 1\3 cup of breadcrumbs
- 0.7 oz parmesan cheese
- Zest of ½ lemon
- Small bunch of parsley
- Salt to taste
- Pepper to taste

Instructions:
Finely chop the parsley and mix it with the breadcrumbs, parmesan, and lemon zest. Season with salt and pepper. Rinse the scallops and top them with the breadcrumb mixture. Bake in the air fryer at 360°F for ten minutes.

MARINATED SQUID

Servings: 2
Difficulty: Low
Cooking Time: 10 minutes

Ingredients:
- 17.6 oz squid
- Olive oil
- 1 lemon
- Small bunch of parsley
- 1 garlic clove
- Pepper to taste

Instructions:
Clean the squid well and make small incisions on the body with a knife.
Finely chop the garlic and parsley and transfer them to a bowl. Add the lemon juice, olive oil, and squid. Season with pepper, mix, and let marinate for about an hour, covered with plastic wrap.
Preheat the air fryer to 390°F for three minutes. Grill the squid at 390°F, cooking for five minutes on each side. Serve with an extra drizzle of extra virgin olive oil.

UMBRINA (MEAGRE) WITH SUN-DRIED TOMATOES, PISTACHIO CRUST, AND ZUCCHINI PESTO

Servings: 2
Difficulty: Low
Cooking Time: 10 minutes

Ingredients:
- 1 Umbrina (Meagre) fish
- 10 sun-dried tomato fillets
- 1\4 cup of pistachios

Zucchini Pesto:
- 1 small zucchini
- 4 tbsp. of extra virgin olive oil
- 3 tbsp of grated Parmesan cheese
- Small bunch of basil

Instructions:
For the pesto: Wash, dry, and trim the zucchini. Grate it and let it sit in a bowl with a pinch of salt for about 30 minutes. Squeeze out the excess water and blend it in a mixer with Parmesan, basil, and oil until smooth. Adjust seasoning and set aside. Clean the fish by removing scales and gutting it. Fillet the fish and place the fillets on perforated parchment paper. Cover them with sun-dried tomatoes and bake at 330°F for ten minutes. Serve the fillets with zucchini pesto and a sprinkle of crushed pistachios.

SWORDFISH SKEWERS WITH PISTACHIO SAUCE AND CARAMELIZED ONIONS

Servings: 2
Difficulty: Medium-High
Cooking Time: 12 minutes

Ingredients:
- 10.6 oz swordfish
- 12 unsalted pistachios
- 1 tsp olive oil
- 1 lemon
- 1 garlic clove
- Salt to taste

Marinade:
- 1 tbsp. of white wine
- Extra virgin olive oil

Breading:
- Breadcrumbs
- 1 tsp of grated Parmesan cheese
- Pinch of salt

Caramelized Onions:
- 3 red onions
- 1 tbsp. white wine vinegar
- 2 tbsp of sugar
- 15 bay leaves
- Olive oil
- Salt to taste

Instructions:
For the pistachio sauce, blend the pistachios with olive oil in a mixer. Peel and thinly slice the onions. Cook them in a pan over very low heat with a drizzle of olive oil, stirring often. Once softened, add a pinch of salt, vinegar, and sugar. Cook for another three minutes until the sugar dissolves. Turn off the heat and let it rest. Wash and pat dry the swordfish. Skin it and cut it into approximately 0.8-inch cubes. In a bowl, mix the squeezed lemon juice, olive oil, white wine, and crushed garlic clove. Add the swordfish cubes and let them marinate for about ten minutes, stirring occasionally. On a plate, mix the breadcrumbs, salt, and a tsp. of grated Parmesan. Drain the swordfish and coat it in the breadcrumb mixture. Skewer the swordfish cubes, alternating with bay leaves. Place them on perforated parchment paper, spray with a bit of oil, and cook at 360°F for 10-12 minutes. Serve the skewers with pistachio sauce and caramelized onions.

CUTTLEFISH AND SQUID BURGER

Servings: 2
Difficulty: Low
Cooking Time: 15 minutes

Ingredients:
- 21 oz cuttlefish
- 1 garlic clove
- 2 cups of green beans
- 15 yellow and red cherry tomatoes
- Small bunch of parsley
- Extra virgin olive oil
- Pepper to taste
- Salt to taste

Instructions:
Trim the green beans, wash them, and boil them. Season with oil and salt.
Wash the tomatoes and quarter them. Season with salt and oil and set aside.
Clean the cuttlefish, wash them, and drain them well.
Blend them in a mixer with pepper, garlic clove, and parsley. The protein released will allow the fish to bind without the need for an egg.
Shape the mixture into hamburgers using a mold or by forming a ball and flattening it with your hands. Place them on squares of parchment paper.
Bake in a preheated air fryer at 370°F for 15 minutes, turning halfway through.
Serve the hamburgers with a salad of cherry tomatoes and boiled green beans.

SEAFOOD BURGER WITH SWORDFISH, SALMON, AND SQUID

Servings: 2
Difficulty: Low
Cooking Time: 15 minutes

Ingredients:
- 1 slice of swordfish
- 1 slice of salmon fillet
- Small bunch of parsley
- 1 squid
- 1 garlic clove
- Extra virgin olive oil
- Pepper to taste

Instructions:
Clean the squid, wash, and drain well.
Place the fish in a mixer along with pepper, garlic clove, and parsley. Blend until combined. Shape the mixture into hamburgers and place them on squares of parchment paper. Bake in a preheated air fryer at 370°F for 15 minutes, turning halfway through. Serve with grilled vegetables or a salad.

CHICKEN ROLLS WITH HAM AND CHEESE

Servings: 2
Difficulty: Medium-High
Cooking Time: 20 minutes

Ingredients:
- 10 thin slices of chicken breast
- 5 slices of cooked ham
- 1 tbsp of grated cheese
- Breadcrumbs to taste
- 10 slices of cheese (Emmental, Scamorza, etc.)
- Salt to taste

Instructions:
On a plate, mix breadcrumbs, a pinch of salt, and grated cheese.
Coat the chicken slices in the breadcrumb mixture and fill them with half a slice of ham and a slice of cheese.
Roll them up and secure them with a skewer.
Spray them with oil and bake at 370°F for ten minutes; turn, spray with a bit more oil, and continue baking for another ten minutes.

CHICKEN ROLL WITH POTATOES

Servings: 2
Difficulty: Medium
Cooking Time: 50 minutes

Ingredients:
- 21.2 oz slices of chicken breast
- 2.8 oz Scamorza cheese
- 1\8 cup of pine nuts
- 2.8 oz Speck (smoked ham)
- 3 sprigs of rosemary
- 1 1\3 cups of spinach
- 3 potatoes
- 3 garlic cloves
- ½ cup of wine
- Extra virgin olive oil
- Paprika
- Salt
- Pepper

Instructions:
Peel the potatoes and cut them into cubes. Soak them in cold water to remove starch.
In a pan, heat some oil and a garlic clove. Add the spinach and cook on low heat. Season with salt and pepper, let it cool and remove the garlic.
Toast the pine nuts.
On a cutting board, lay out the slightly beaten chicken slices, overlapping slightly. Fill them with spinach, pine nuts, cheese slices, and Speck. Roll them up and tie them with cooking twine.
Place the rolled chicken in a baking dish, add a garlic clove and a sprig of rosemary, and bake at 360°F for 30 minutes, turning often. Drain the potatoes and season with oil, salt, pepper, paprika, grated cheese, and wine. Mix well and bake at 360°F for 20 minutes, shaking occasionally for even cooking.

BREADED CHICKEN WINGS

Servings: 2
Difficulty: Low
Cooking Time: 25 minutes

Ingredients:
- 10 chicken wings
- Garlic powder
- 3 tbsp of breadcrumbs
- 1 tbsp of grated parmesan cheese
- Paprika

Instructions:
Rinse the chicken wings and remove any feathers. Pat dry with paper towels. On a plate, combine breadcrumbs, cheese, garlic powder, and paprika. Coat the chicken wings in the mixture and fry at 390°F for 25 minutes.

POTATOES AND BACON

Servings: 4
Difficulty: Low
Cooking Time: 20 minutes

Ingredients:
- 3 cups of new potatoes
- 1 sprig of rosemary
- 3.5 oz thin slices of bacon
- Extra virgin olive oil
- Salt to taste
- Pepper to taste

Instructions:
Finely chop the rosemary.
Wash the potatoes and boil them with their skin on for about ten minutes. They should be soft when pierced with a fork but not falling apart. Drain and season with salt, pepper, and olive oil. Mix gently and let them cool slightly.
Cut the bacon slices in half and wrap them around the potatoes.
Place them in a baking dish and bake at 390°F for about 20 minutes.

MEAT FLAN

Servings: 8-inch pan
Difficulty: Low
Cooking Time: 25 minutes

Ingredients:
- 12.3 oz ground turkey
- 10 pitted black olives
- 3.5 oz Speck (smoked ham)
- Extra virgin olive oil
- 1\3 cup of tomato concentrate
- 1.8 oz grated Parmesan cheese
- 3.5 oz mozzarella cheese
- 1 garlic clove
- 2 zucchinis
- Smoked paprika
- 1 egg
- Pepper to taste
- Salt to taste

Instructions:
Wash, trim, and grate the zucchini. Season with some salt and let them rest to release water.
In a bowl, combine the ground turkey, cheese, egg, tomato concentrate, paprika, and finely chopped garlic. Add the zucchinis, squeezing out their water, and season with salt and pepper. Mix well.
Grease a baking dish with oil and spread half of the mixture, pressing it down. Layer with mozzarella slices, olive slices, and Speck. Cover with the remaining meat mixture and press down slightly.
Bake in the air fryer at 360°F for 25 minutes.

ALMOND-CRUSTED UMBRINA

Servings: 2
Difficulty: Low
Cooking Time: 15 minutes

Ingredients:
- 4 Umbrina fillets
- 4 slices of bread
- Extra virgin olive oil
- 1\3 cup of sun-dried tomatoes
- Small bunch of parsley
- 1 tbsp of capers
- 1\3 cup of almonds
- Garlic powder
- Pepper to taste

Instructions:
Drain the sun-dried tomatoes and place them in a mixer with bread, capers, parsley, and almonds. Blend until combined. Season with pepper and garlic powder.
Spread the mixture on the Umbrina fillets placed on perforated parchment paper. Bake in the air fryer at 360°F for 15 minutes.

CHICKEN TAGLIATA WITH VALERIAN, ALMONDS, MANGO, AND AVOCADO

Servings: 2
Difficulty: Low
Cooking Time: 30 minutes

Ingredients:
- 1 whole chicken breast
- 2 sprigs of rosemary
- 1 tbsp of pink
- Valerian (lamb's lettuce)
- peppercorns
- ½ mango
- Extra virgin olive oil
- ½ avocado
- 1 lemon
- 1 tsp of paprika
- ½ tsp of garlic powder
- ½ Tbsp. of curry
- Salt to taste
- Black pepper to taste

Instructions:
Marinate the whole chicken in a bowl with the juice of ½ lemon, paprika, crushed pink peppercorns, garlic powder, curry, rosemary sprigs, and a drizzle of oil. Massage well to distribute the spices and let them rest covered for about three hours. After this time, cook the whole piece at 390°F for 30 minutes.
Meanwhile, wash the valerian and place it on a serving plate. Peel the mango and avocado and cut them into small cubes, adding them to the valerian.
In a glass, squeeze the remaining lemon, add a pinch of salt and some oil, then whisk vigorously to form a vinaigrette. Slice the chicken diagonally into small slices and lay them on the prepared salad. Dress with the vinaigrette, and serve.

CHICKEN PARCELS WITH SPICES

Servings: 2
Difficulty: Low
Cooking Time: 25 minutes

Ingredients:
- 4 chicken thighs
- Garlic
- 3.5 oz grated cheese
- Sage
- 5-6 taralli (Italian crackers)
- Ginger to taste
- Extra virgin olive oil
- 1 sprig of rosemary
- Salt
- Pepper

Instructions:
Remove the skin and bones from the thighs and lightly beat them.
In a mixer, grind the taralli with the rosemary sprig. Add garlic, salt, pepper, and cheese, and mix.
Cut pieces of parchment paper, lightly grease them with olive oil, and place a thigh in the center. Sprinkle with the prepared mixture, grate some ginger, and finish with a sage leaf.
Close the parcel, ensuring the sides are tucked underneath to prevent the paper from lifting and burning during cooking. Cook everything at 390°F for 20 minutes.
Serve directly in the parcel.

FARMER'S EGGS

Servings: 2
Difficulty: Low
Cooking Time: 7 minutes

Ingredients:
- 2 eggs
- 2 slices of smoked scamorza cheese
- Pepper to taste
- 2\3 cups of spinach
- 1 garlic clove
- 1.8 oz grated Parmesan cheese
- Extra virgin olive oil
- Salt to taste

Instructions:
Blanch the spinach if fresh and sauté in a pan with a garlic clove and a drizzle of oil. If using frozen spinach, sauté directly in the pan with oil and garlic. Season with salt and pepper, and remove the garlic.
Use individual ramekins, grease with a bit of oil, and place the spinach at the bottom, followed by the smoked scamorza then the egg.
Sprinkle with Parmesan. Cook at 360°F for seven minutes.

EGGS WITH ZUCCHINI

Servings: 2
Difficulty: Low
Cooking Time: 7 minutes

Ingredients:
- 3 eggs
- 3 zucchinis
- 1 garlic clove
- 2.1 oz grated Parmesan cheese
- Extra virgin olive oil
- Pepper to taste
- Salt to taste

Instructions:
Wash and trim the zucchinis, then slice them. In a pan, sauté the garlic with a drizzle of oil and add the zucchini. Cook on low heat with the lid on for ten minutes. Let it cool slightly.
Grease two ramekins with a bit of oil and place the zucchinis at the bottom.
Break an egg into a bowl, season with salt, pepper, and cheese, whisk well, and pour over the zucchini. Cook in the air fryer at 360°F for seven minutes.

BREAD AND MORTADELLA BALLS

Servings: 4
Difficulty: Low
Cooking Time: 20 minutes

Ingredients:
- 2 eggs
- 7 oz Mortadella
- 1.4 oz grated pecorino cheese
- Vegetable oil
- 1 oz grated parmesan cheese
- 14.1 oz stale bread
- Small bunch of parsley
- Milk as needed
- Breadcrumbs as needed
- Salt to taste
- Pepper to taste

Instructions:
In a bowl, soak the stale bread in milk.
Squeeze out the excess milk and place the bread in a bowl. Season with salt, pepper, cheese, eggs, and finely chopped parsley. Slice the Mortadella very thinly and add it to the mixture. Form balls, roll them in breadcrumbs, spray them with oil spray, and place them on the fryer's grill on perforated parchment paper.
Cook at 360°F for 15-20 minutes, turning halfway through.

ZUCCHINI WITH RICOTTA AND BASIL

Servings: 2
Difficulty: Low
Cooking Time: 25 minutes

Ingredients:
- 2 zucchinis
- 1 egg
- 10 basil leaves
- 8.8 oz ricotta cheese
- Extra virgin olive oil
- 1.8 oz grated parmesan cheese
- 2 tbsp of breadcrumbs
- Salt to taste
- Pepper to taste

Instructions:
In a bowl, combine ricotta, grated cheese, breadcrumbs, egg, pepper, salt, and finely chopped basil.
Wash the zucchinis, dry them, and cut them in half. Hollow out the center, season with a drizzle of oil and pepper, and stuff with the ricotta and basil cream.
Sprinkle the surface with more breadcrumbs, a drizzle of oil, and a pinch of salt, and bake at 380°F for about 25 minutes.

MARINATED TURKEY

Servings: 2
Difficulty: Low
Cooking Time: 20 minutes

Ingredients:
- 14 oz turkey breast
- 1 sprig of rosemary
- Some chive tufts
- sprig of oregano
- Pepper to taste
- Some sprigs of thyme
- Extra virgin olive oil
- 2 sage leaves
- 1 lemon
- Salt to taste

Instructions:
In a dish, squeeze the lemon, and add salt, pepper, and finely chopped herbs. Add some oil and whisk everything together until the salt dissolves and everything is combined.
Lay the turkey slices in the liquid and marinate for a couple of hours, turning halfway through to flavor both sides.
Cook at 380°F for 20 minutes, turning halfway through.
Serve the turkey breast with a salad or vegetables of your choice.

ROLLS WITH ZUCCHINI, SPECK, AND PHILADELPHIA ON PANCARRÈ

Servings: 2
Difficulty: Low
Cooking Time: 21 minutes

Ingredients:
- 2 small zucchinis
- 4 slices of long sandwich bread
- Philadelphia cream cheese
- 1 egg
- 8 slices of speck (smoked ham)
- Breadcrumbs

Instructions:
Wash the zucchinis, trim the ends, and slice them. Spray them with a bit of oil spray. Cook at 380°F for seven minutes on the air fryer grill.
Flatten the sandwich bread slices with a rolling pin to prevent them from breaking when rolling.
Spread the slices with cream cheese, and layer with grilled zucchinis and speck. Roll them tightly and cut each bread roll into 3 parts.
Beat the egg with a fork and dip the rolls first in the egg, then in the breadcrumbs.
Cook the rolls on the air fryer grill covered with perforated parchment paper at 370°F for 15 minutes.

ROSEMARY-INFUSED PORK RIBS

Servings: 2
Difficulty: Low
Cooking Time: 20 minutes

Ingredients:
- 4 pork ribs
- 1 sprig of rosemary
- Pepper to taste
- ½ tsp of garlic powder
- 1 tbsp of spicy paprika
- Salt to taste

Instructions:
Wash and finely chop the rosemary. Combine it with garlic powder, paprika, pepper, and a pinch of salt. Coat the ribs on both sides with the spice mix and grill in the air fryer at 390°F for 20 minutes, turning halfway through. Note: To prevent the dripping fat from smoking, add half a cup of water to the fryer basket. (Always read the instructions for your air fryer).

ORANGE GLAZED SALMON

Servings: 2
Difficulty: Low
Cooking Time: 10 minutes

Ingredients:
- 4 salmon fillets
- 1 tsp of mustard
- 1 orange
- 2 tbsp of orange marmalade
- Salt to taste
- Pepper to taste

Instructions:
Grate the orange zest and squeeze its juice. In a bowl, combine the orange marmalade, grated zest, and mustard. Mix with the orange juice using a fork.
Season the fillets with salt and pepper, and brush them with the sauce. Place the salmon fillets on a piece of parchment paper, fold it to seal, ensuring the folded part is at the bottom, and place the parcel in a baking dish. Cook at 390°F for ten minutes, gently turning halfway through.
Serve the salmon with sautéed spinach or other preferred vegetables.

GRATIN SCALLOPS

Servings: 2
Difficulty: Low
Cooking Time: 13 minutes

Ingredients:
- 4 scallops
- 1\3 cup of breadcrumbs
- 1 tsp of grated cheese
- Garlic powder
- Small bunch of parsley
- Extra virgin olive oil
- Zest of ½ lemon
- Pepper to taste
- Salt to taste

Instructions:
In a bowl, combine cheese, breadcrumbs, garlic powder, lemon zest, and finely chopped parsley. Mix with a fork. Add a drizzle of oil and mix until crumbs form.
Place the scallops on your fryer's grill and top them with the breadcrumb mixture. sprinkle some salt and pepper on top. Cook at 360°F for 13 minutes.

PISTACHIO-CRUSTED SCALLOPS

Servings: 2
Difficulty: Low
Cooking Time: 13 minutes

Ingredients:
- 4 scallops
- Small bunch of parsley
- 1\4 cup of pistachios
- Extra virgin olive oil
- 1 tsp of grated cheese
- Salt to taste
- 2 tbsp of breadcrumbs

Instructions:
In a mixer, combine pistachios, cheese, breadcrumbs, and parsley. Blend until finely chopped. Add a drizzle of oil and a little salt, and mix until crumbs form.
Place the scallops on your fryer's grill and top them with the pistachio breadcrumb mixture. Cook at 360°F for 13 minutes.

SPECK-WRAPPED SCALLOPS

Servings: 2
Difficulty: Low
Cooking Time: 12 minutes

Ingredients:
- 12 scallops
- Pink peppercorns
- 12 slices of speck (smoked ham)
- 2 bay leaves
- Extra virgin olive oil
- 1 garlic clove
- ½ cup of brandy

Instructions:
Gently detach the scallops from their shells. Wrap each scallop with a slice of speck and secure them with a long skewer, threading three scallops per skewer.
Place them in a baking dish with a drizzle of oil. Add the crushed garlic clove, bay leaves, and pink peppercorns. Cook at 360°F for five minutes.
Add the brandy and continue cooking for another seven minutes.

EGGPLANT PARMIGIANA

Servings: 4
Difficulty: Low
Cooking Time: 51 minutes

Ingredients:
- 2 small eggplants
- 3.5 oz mozzarella cheese
- 1 3\4 cups of tomato sauce
- 1.8 oz Parmesan cheese
- 1 1\3 cups of béchamel sauce
- 3 basil leaves
- ½ small onion
- Extra virgin olive oil
- Salt to taste

Instructions:
Wash, trim, and slice the eggplants. Place them in a dish, drizzle with oil, and mix well. Grill the eggplants in the air fryer at 360°F for 11 minutes. To expedite the cooking process, you can skewer them, leaving space between slices.
In a pot, prepare the sauce: add some oil and thinly sliced onion. Once the onion is slightly browned, add the tomato sauce, cover, and simmer for about 30 minutes, stirring occasionally. Turn off the heat, add basil, cover, and let it rest.
Take a ladle of sauce and mix it with the béchamel. Spread another ladle of sauce at the base of a baking dish. Layer the eggplants, slightly overlapping, followed by a thin layer of pink béchamel, crumbled mozzarella, and a sprinkle of Parmesan.
Repeat layers, finishing with sauce and grated cheese on top.
Bake at 360°F for ten minutes.

BEEF TAGLIATA

Servings: 2
Difficulty: Low
Cooking Time: 8 minutes

Ingredients:
- 10.6 oz beef steak (2 slices)
- 1 oz Parmesan cheese shavings
- ½ cup of arugula
- 2 tbsp balsamic vinegar
- ½ cup of cherry tomatoes
- Extra virgin olive oil
- Coarse salt to taste

Instructions:
Spray the steaks with some oil, add a pinch of coarse salt, and massage both sides.
Wash and quarter the cherry tomatoes, place them in a bowl, season with salt, add oil, and let them rest.
Grill the steaks at 370°F for eight minutes, turning halfway through.
Serve the steaks topped with arugula, tomatoes with their juice, Parmesan shavings, drizzled with balsamic vinegar, and a splash of oil. Adjust the cooking time based on your preferred doneness.

PORK CAPOCOLLO GRATIN

Servings: 2
Difficulty: Low
Cooking Time: 20 minutes

Ingredients:
- 2 slices of capocollo
- 2 tbsp of Parmesan cheese
- 1 garlic clove
- 1\4 cup of breadcrumbs
- ½ tbsp of paprika
- Extra virgin olive oil
- Small bunch of parsley
- Salt to taste

Instructions:
In a mixer, blend garlic and parsley. Transfer to a bowl and add breadcrumbs, paprika, and cheese. Mix with a fork. Drizzle with oil and mix until crumbs form.
Place the capocollo on the air fryer grill and cover with the breadcrumb mixture. Cook at 380°F for 20 minutes.

CHICKEN LEGS WITH SPECK

Servings: 2
Difficulty: Low
Cooking Time: 30 minutes

Ingredients:
- 6 boneless chicken legs
- 1 garlic clove
- 6 slices of speck (smoked ham)
- 2 bay leaves
- Olives
- Extra virgin olive oil
- ½ cup of white wine

Instructions:
Wrap the boneless chicken with speck and place them in a baking dish. Spray with some oil and cook at 370°F for ten minutes, turning frequently.
Add the crushed garlic clove, bay leaves, white wine, and olives. Continue cooking at 380°F for another 20 minutes.

SUPER PIZZAIOLA CHICKEN WITH ROASTED POTATOES

Servings: 2
Difficulty: Low
Cooking Time: 38 minutes

Ingredients:
- 1 cup of potatoes
- 1 garlic clove
- 6 chicken wings
- 3 bay leaves
- Extra virgin olive oil
- 1 handful of capers
- 1 small celery stalk
- ½ cup of white wine
- ½ onion
- 2 large tomatoes for sauce

Instructions:
Peel and cut the potatoes into wedges. Soak them in cold water for an hour. Drain and dry the potatoes using a towel. Spray with oil and cook on the air fryer grill at 380°F for 20 minutes, shaking occasionally for even cooking.
In a baking dish (for the fryer), brown the chicken wings on all sides.
Finely chop garlic, onion, and celery stalk. Add to the chicken along with capers, bay leaves, and diced tomatoes. Add wine and continue cooking for another ten minutes.
Add the potatoes, gently mix to flavor them, and cook at 360°F for another seven to eight minutes.

SPINACH-STUFFED GROUND MEAT ROLL

Servings: 2
Difficulty: Low
Cooking Time: 25 minutes

Ingredients:
- 12.3 oz ground meat
- 3.5 oz parmesan cheese
- 1 cup of spinach
- 1 garlic clove
- 1 tbsp of breadcrumbs
- Extra virgin olive oil
- 1 egg
- Salt to taste
- Pepper to taste

Instructions:
In a pan with some oil, add the crushed garlic and sauté the spinach. Season with salt and let it cool.
In a bowl, combine ground meat, cheese, breadcrumbs, egg, salt, and pepper. Mix well with your hands.
On a parchment paper, spread the meat to form a 0.4-inch thick rectangle. Fill with spinach and, using the paper, roll it up. Seal the ends and place it in a baking dish. Cook at 390°F for 20 minutes, turning halfway through. Let it cool slightly and cut into approximately 0.6-inch slices. Serve with a side salad.

MORTADELLA AND PISTACHIO GROUND MEAT ROLL

Servings: 2
Difficulty: Low
Cooking Time: 25 minutes

Ingredients:
- 12.3 oz ground meat
- 1 cup of spinach
- 3 slices of mortadella
- 1 garlic clove
- 1 Tbsp. of breadcrumbs
- Extra virgin olive oil
- 1 egg
- 5.3 oz crushed pistachios
- 3.5 oz Parmesan cheese
- Salt to taste
- Pepper to taste

Instructions:
In a pan with some oil, add the crushed garlic and sauté the spinach. Season with salt and let it cool.
In a bowl, combine ground meat, cheese, breadcrumbs, egg, salt, and pepper. Mix well with your hands.
On parchment paper, spread the meat to form a 0.4-inch thick rectangle. Fill with spinach and mortadella slices. Using the paper, roll it up, then roll it in the crushed pistachios to coat.
Spray with oil, wrap it in the paper and seal. Cook at 390°F for 20 minutes, turning occasionally. Let it cool slightly and cut into approximately 0.6-inch slices. Serve with oven-roasted potatoes.

CITRUS-MARINATED SALMON

Servings: 2
Difficulty: Low
Cooking Time: 13 minutes

Ingredients:
- 2 fresh salmon fillets
- 1 tsp. of cornstarch
- 2 tbsp of tomato paste
- 1 bunch of dill
- 1 garlic clove
- ½ cup of white wine
- Extra virgin olive oil
- Pepper to taste
- Salt to taste

Instructions:
Wash and dry the salmon. Season with salt and pepper. Mix the tomato paste in the wine and add the cornstarch, stirring to dissolve. Transfer to a dish, add dill, garlic, and a splash of oil. Marinate for about 1 hour.
Preheat the fryer to 370°F for three minutes. Place the fillets skin-side down on the grill and cook for about 13 minutes.

SALT-BAKED CHICKEN

Servings: 2
Difficulty: Low
Cooking Time: 50 minutes

Ingredients:
- 21.2 oz whole chicken
- 2.2 lb. of coarse salt

Instructions:
Create a 0.4-0.8 inch layer of salt in the basket. Place the chicken on it and cover with salt.
Spray with some water to compact and bake at 360°F for 50 minutes. Let it cool for a few minutes, then break the salt crust and remove the chicken. Clean it from any remaining salt and serve with a mixed salad.

ROSEMARY-INFUSED SALT-BAKED CHICKEN

Servings: 2
Difficulty: Low
Cooking Time: 50 minutes

Ingredients:
- 21.2 oz whole chicken
- 3 sprigs of rosemary
- 2.2 lb. of coarse salt

Instructions:
Create a 0.4-0.8 inch layer of salt in the basket. Crumble a sprig of rosemary on it, place the chicken, add the other rosemary sprigs, and cover with salt. Spray with some water to compact and bake at 360°F for 50 minutes. Let it cool for a few minutes, break the salt crust, and remove the chicken. Clean it from any remaining salt and serve on a bed of salad.

CITRUS-INFUSED SALT-BAKED CHICKEN

Servings: 2
Difficulty: Low
Cooking Time: 50 minutes

Ingredients:
- 21.2 oz of whole chicken
- 3 fennels
- 1\3 cup of coarse salt
- Olive oil as needed
- 1 untreated lemon
- 3 tbsp of balsamic vinegar
- 2 untreated oranges

Instructions:
Wash and slice the lemon and orange.
Create a 0.4-0.8 inch layer of salt in the basket and place some lemon and orange slices at the base.
Position the chicken, add the remaining orange and lemon slices, and cover with salt.
Spray with some water to compact and bake at 360°F for 50 minutes.
Thoroughly wash the fennel and slice it. Peel the orange and slice it.
Combine the orange with the fennel season with salt, olive oil, and balsamic vinegar.
Let the chicken cool for a few minutes before breaking the salt crust. Clean it from any remaining salt and serve with the fennel and orange salad.

SALT-BAKED SEA BREAM

Servings: 2
Difficulty: Low
Cooking Time: 30 minutes

Ingredients:
- 14.1 oz sea bream
- ½ lemon
- 1\3 cup of coarse salt

Instructions:
Clean the fish well by removing the innards and rinsing thoroughly.
Slice the lemon.
In the basket, create a base with the salt, place some lemon slices, and lay the fish on top. Add a few more lemon slices and cover the fish with salt, leaving only the head exposed. Cook at 360°F for 30 minutes.

BEER-MARINATED CHICKEN

Servings: 2
Difficulty: Low
Cooking Time: 35 minutes

Ingredients:
- 4 boneless chicken thighs
- 3 sage leaves
- Salt, as needed
- 3 bay leaves
- 2 garlic cloves
- 1 cup of beer
- 2 sprigs of rosemary
- 2 tbsp of extra virgin olive oil
- Pepper, as needed
- Flour, as needed

Instructions:
Season the chicken thighs with salt and pepper on a cutting board.
Crush the garlic cloves and place them in a dish with rosemary, sage, and bay leaves.
Add the chicken and cover with beer. Marinate, covered, for at least an hour.
After marinating, coat the chicken in flour and place it in a pan.
Strain the liquid and set aside. Brown the chicken on all sides for about ten minutes.
Add the marinade liquid and cook in the fryer at 360°F for 25 minutes. The beer should almost completely evaporate, forming a crust.

ROASTED CHICKEN

Servings: 2
Difficulty: Low
Cooking Time: 25 minutes

Ingredients:
- 17.6 oz chicken pieces
- 1 lemon
- 2 garlic cloves
- 2 sprigs of rosemary
- Olive oil, as needed
- Salt

Instructions:
Coarsely chop the garlic and rosemary and slice the lemon.
Massage the chicken pieces with oil and season with salt. Place them in a freezer bag, and add lemon slices, garlic, and rosemary. Seal and let it rest overnight in the fridge.
In the fryer basket, pour some water and place the grill. (If your fryer's grill has very low feet, raise it on a pan and pour the water into the pan itself. This will prevent the chicken fat from burning and producing smoke.) Set the fryer to 390°F for 20-25 minutes.

AROMATIZED SALTED CHICKEN

Servings: 2
Difficulty: Low
Cooking Time: 50 minutes

Ingredients:
- 21.2 oz whole chicken
- 2 sprigs of thyme
- 1\3 cup of coarse salt
- 3 sage leaves
- 3 sprigs of rosemary
- 1 garlic clove

Instructions:
Clean and crush the garlic clove. Insert it inside the chicken along with a sprig of rosemary, thyme, and a sage leaf. Create a 0.4-0.8 inch layer of salt in the basket. Crumble the remaining herbs (rosemary, thyme, and sage), then place the chicken on top and cover it with salt.
Spray some water to compact the salt and bake at 360°F for 50 minutes.
Allow the chicken to cool for a few minutes, break the salt crust, clean it from any remaining salt, and serve with grilled potatoes or vegetables.

SQUID AND PEAS

Servings: 2
Difficulty: Low
Cooking Time: 35 minutes

Ingredients:
- 1 1\3 cups of peas
- 17.6 oz squid
- 1 onion
- 1 cup of cherry tomatoes
- ½ cup of white wine
- 1 garlic clove
- Extra virgin olive oil
- A small bunch of parsley
- Salt

Instructions:
Clean the squid thoroughly, removing the innards, and also remove the eyes and mouth from the head. Rinse well and slice into rings.
In a pan with some oil, add the garlic clove, finely chopped parsley, onion, and peas. Cook in a fryer at 360°F for ten minutes. Add the wine and cook for another five minutes. If it becomes too dry, add some broth or water.
Wash and quarter the cherry tomatoes. Add them along with the squid to the peas. Cook everything together at 360°F for 20 minutes.

CUTTLEFISH STEAK

Servings: 2
Difficulty: Low
Cooking Time: 15 minutes

Ingredients:
- 24.7 oz cuttlefish
- 3\4 cup of cherry tomatoes
- 1.8 oz grated cheese
- 2 tsp of balsamic vinegar
- Olive oil
- A small bunch of arugula
- Pepper to taste
- Salt to taste

Instructions:
Clean the cuttlefish thoroughly, leaving them whole, and remove the eyes and mouth from the head.
Spray the cuttlefish with oil and place them on the grill; cook at 370°F for 15 minutes, turning halfway through. Wash the cherry tomatoes and quarter them. Season with salt, pepper, and oil.
Slice the cuttlefish into strips and arrange them on a serving plate. Add arugula, cherry tomatoes with their juice, and grated cheese. Season with a pinch of salt, a sprinkle of pepper, a drizzle of oil, and balsamic vinegar.

VEAL ROLLS WITH PEAS IN WHITE SAUCE

Servings: 2
Difficulty: Low
Cooking Time: 40 minutes

Ingredients:
- 17.6 oz veal slices
- 5.3 oz cooked ham
- 1 cup of peas
- 2.8 oz fontina cheese
- 1 onion
- 1 carrot
- 1 cup of broth
- Extra virgin olive oil
- Salt to taste

Instructions:
Lay out the veal slices on a flat surface. If they are large, cut them in half.
Stuff the slices with ham and cheese, roll them up, secure the edges, and skewer them with toothpicks to prevent them from opening during cooking.
In a small pan with some oil, add finely chopped onion, carrot, and peas. Cook over low heat for six minutes.
Add a cup of broth and cook in a fryer at 370°F for ten minutes. Add the veal rolls and cook for another 15-20 minutes. If it dries out too much, add another half cup of broth.

VEAL ROLLS WITH MORTADELLA AND PROVOLONE CHEESE

Servings: 2
Difficulty: Low
Cooking Time: 30 minutes

Ingredients:
- 21.2 oz veal slices
- 3 carrots
- 4.2 oz mortadella
- Extra virgin olive oil
- 3.5 oz provolone cheese
- ½ cup broth
- 1 onion
- Flour as needed

Instructions:
Lay out the veal slices on a flat surface and fill them with mortadella and provolone. Close and secure with toothpicks.
Coat the rolls in flour, shaking off the excess, and brown them in a pan over low heat with a drizzle of oil.
Peel and dice the carrots. Clean and thinly slice the onion.
Sauté the carrots, onion, and rolls over low heat for five minutes.
Transfer everything to a small pan, add half a cup of broth, and continue cooking in the fryer at 370°F for 20 minutes.

LAMB CHOPS

Servings: 2
Difficulty: Low
Cooking Time: 15 minutes

Ingredients:
- 4 lamb chops
- A small bunch of parsley
- Bread crumbs
- 1 tsp. of paprika
- Cheese
- Garlic
- Extra virgin olive oil
- Salt to taste

Instructions:
Finely chop garlic and parsley and place them in a dish. Add cheese, paprika, and bread crumbs, and mix.
Spray the lamb chops with oil, sprinkle with a pinch of salt and massage. Coat them in the breadcrumb mixture, and cook on the fryer grill at 390°F for 15 minutes, turning halfway through and spraying again with oil.

POTATO NESTS WITH MUSHROOMS AND SAUSAGE

Servings: 4
Difficulty: Low
Cooking Time: 20 minutes

Ingredients:
- 2 cups of potatoes
- 2 eggs
- 1\3 cup of butter
- 1.8 oz grated cheese
- Salt to taste
- Pepper to taste

For the filling:
- 1 cup of mixed mushrooms
- 12.3 oz sausage
- Extra virgin olive oil
- 1 garlic clove
- Butter as needed
- Bread crumbs as needed

Instructions:
Wash the potatoes thoroughly. Boil them with their skin on until they are tender when pierced with a fork.
Clean the mushrooms. In a pan with some oil, brown the crushed garlic clove. Add the mushrooms and sausage (removed from its casing), and cook covered for ten minutes. Uncover, let the liquid evaporate, and allow it to cool. Peel the potatoes while still warm, mash them, and transfer them to a bowl. Add butter, cheese, eggs, salt, and pepper, then mix. Place the mixture in a piping bag with a star nozzle.
Butter some aluminum molds and sprinkle them with bread crumbs. Starting from the center, create a spiral with the potato mixture, filling the bottom and only going up the sides to create a nest. Fill with the sausage and mushroom mixture, and sprinkle with Parmesan cheese. Cook at 360°F for 20 minutes.

SAUSAGE, BACON, AND ZUCCHINI ROLLS

Servings: 2
Difficulty: Low
Cooking Time: 35 minutes

Ingredients:
- 6 large sausage slices
- 1 zucchini
- 12 bacon slices
- Extra virgin olive oil

Instructions:
Wash and trim the zucchini, slice it, spray with oil, and grill at 360°F for nine minutes.
Cut the sausages in half, wrap them with zucchini and bacon, skewer them, and grill at 380°F for 25 minutes. Serve with a mixed salad and very thin slices of raw onion.

MEAT SKEWERS WITH VEGETABLES

Servings: 2
Difficulty: Low
Cooking Time: 30 minutes

Ingredients:
- 7 oz pork
- 7 oz beef
- 5.3 oz chicken
- Olive oil
- 5.3 oz sausage
- A bunch of rosemary
- ½ yellow bell pepper
- 1 onion
- ½ red bell pepper
- Salt to taste
- Pepper to taste

Instructions:
Cut the meat and bell peppers into pieces. Peel the onion, cut it in half, and separate all the layers.
Skewer the meat, alternating the different types of meat and spacing them with colorful vegetable pieces.
Brush with a little oil and season with salt, pepper and chopped rosemary.
Place them on the air fryer grill and roast at 380°F for about 20 minutes, turning occasionally for even cooking.
Adjust cooking time based on the size of the meat pieces.

STUFFED BELL PEPPERS WITH RICOTTA AND SPINACH

Servings: 2
Difficulty: Low
Cooking Time: 30 minutes

Ingredients:
- 2 bell peppers
- 8.8 oz mozzarella cheese
- 1 cup of spinach
- egg
- Pepper to taste
- 1.8 oz grated Parmesan cheese
- Extra virgin olive oil
- 8.8 oz ricotta cheese
- Salt to taste

Instructions:
In a pan with a drizzle of oil, sauté the spinach for about ten minutes. Season with salt and pepper and let it cool.
In a blender, combine mozzarella, spinach, ricotta, egg, and Parmesan, and blend.
Wash and halve the bell peppers. Fill them with the mixture and place them in a baking dish with a drizzle of oil. Sprinkle with some Parmesan and bake at 350°F for 30 minutes.

CHICKEN ROLL IN PUFF PASTRY

Servings: 2
Difficulty: Low
Cooking Time: 35 minutes

Ingredients:
- 1 puff pastry roll
- 8.8 oz mozzarella cheese
- 5 chicken breast slices
- 1 garlic clove
- 1 cup of spinach
- 5.3 oz speck (smoked ham)
- Pepper to taste
- 1.8 oz grated Parmesan cheese
- Salt to taste

Instructions:
In a pan with a drizzle of oil and garlic, cook the spinach. Season with salt and let it cool. Remove the garlic clove. Chop the mozzarella.
Unroll the puff pastry and leave it on its parchment paper.
On a flat surface, slightly overlap the chicken slices. Spread the spinach, mozzarella, and Parmesan on top and gently roll it up. Wrap the speck slices around the roll and then wrap it in the puff pastry. Seal the ends well and place them underneath. Place it on a baking tray lined with parchment paper and bake at 360°F for 35 minutes.

SALMON, CHERRY TOMATO, AND ARUGULA BREAD BOWLS

Servings: 2
Difficulty: Low
Cooking Time: 13 minutes

Ingredients:
- 6 slices of bread (similar to white bread)
- A bunch of arugula
- 12.3 oz salmon
- 20 cherry tomatoes
- Extra virgin olive oil
- Salt and pepper to taste

Instructions:
Flatten the bread slices slightly with a rolling pin to make them more pliable.
Use individual aluminum molds, turn them upside down, and shape the bread slices over them to create a bowl shape. Spray with some oil and bake in the air fryer at 350°F for eight minutes.
In a non-stick pan, sear the salmon. Once cooked, let it cool, remove any bones, skin it, and cut it into cubes.
Wash and quarter the cherry tomatoes. In a bowl, combine the salmon pieces, hand-torn arugula, a drizzle of oil, salt and a grind of pepper. Let the flavors meld.
Fill the bread bowls just before serving to prevent them from breaking.

SALMON PASTRY PARCELS

Servings: 2
Difficulty: Low
Cooking Time: 30 minutes

Ingredients:
- 2 salmon fillets
- ½ cup of spinach
- Extra virgin olive oil
- 1 rectangular puff pastry roll
- 1 garlic clove
- Pepper to taste
- Salt to taste

Instructions:
Check the salmon fillets for bones and remove any with tweezers. Rinse and let them drain in a colander.
In a pan with some oil and garlic, cook the spinach. Once cooked, season with salt, remove the garlic, add some pepper, and let it cool.
Unroll the puff pastry and divide it in two.
Place some spinach in the center of each pastry rectangle, followed by the salmon fillets, and cover with the remaining spinach. Seal the pastry well.
Ensure the seal is at the bottom, and place the fillets on a baking tray lined with parchment paper. Bake at 370°F for about 30 minutes.

SALMON AND POTATO BAKE

Servings: 2
Difficulty: Low
Cooking Time: 30 minutes

Ingredients:
- 2 salmon fillets
- Extra virgin olive oil
- 1 potato
- 1 Tbsp. of paprika
- ½ tsp of powdered paprika
- Salt to taste
- Pepper to taste

Instructions:
Rinse the salmon fillets, check for bones, remove any with tweezers, and pat dry with kitchen paper.
Peel the potato and thinly slice it using a mandolin.
Rinse the potato slices well, drain, place them in a bowl, and season with oil, salt, pepper, paprika, and garlic. Mix well. Spray the salmon fillets with oil and place them on the fryer grill. Cover the fillets with overlapping potato slices, spray with some more oil, and cook at 360°F for 30 minutes.

STUFFED TURKEY ROLLS

Servings: 2
Difficulty: Medium
Cooking Time: 20 minutes

Ingredients:
- 6 turkey thigh slices
- 1 tbsp of capers
- 6 slices of cooked ham
- 2.1 oz provola cheese
- 1 1\2 tbsp of white wine
- 2.1 oz sun-dried tomatoes
- Extra virgin olive oil

Instructions:
Flatten the turkey slices using a meat mallet or a glass.
Drain the sun-dried tomatoes (if in oil) and chop them along with the capers. Chop the provolone cheese as well and set aside.
Cover each turkey slice with a slice of ham and a spoonful of the mixture. Roll tightly and secure with toothpicks.
Place the rolls in a baking dish with some oil and cook at 370°F for five minutes, turning to seal the meat.
Add the wine and continue cooking at 365°F for an additional 15 minutes.

TURKEY ROLLS WITH ASPARAGUS AND SPECK

Servings: 2
Difficulty: Medium
Cooking Time: 20 minutes

Ingredients:
- 6 turkey thigh slices
- 25 asparagus
- 0.4 oz provolone cheese
- 6 speck slices
- Extra virgin olive oil to taste

Instructions:
Wash the asparagus, remove the woody part, and blanch them in salted water. Drain and cut 18 tips to a length of 3.1 inches, setting them aside.
Chop the remaining asparagus and sauté them in a pan with some oil and a garlic clove for five minutes. Blend the sautéed asparagus, adding a little oil and water, if needed, to make a sauce. Season with salt.
Flatten the turkey slices using a meat mallet or a glass.
Cover each turkey slice with a slice of speck, two slices of provolone cheese, and three asparagus tips. Roll tightly and secure with toothpicks.
Grill the rolls, spraying with oil spray, at 380°F for ten minutes. Turn, spray with oil on the other side, and continue cooking at 380°F for another ten minutes.
Serve the turkey rolls with the asparagus sauce.

BAKED COD WITH POTATOES AND OLIVES

Servings: 2
Difficulty: Medium
Cooking Time: 40 minutes

Ingredients:
- 12.3 oz pre-soaked cod
- Extra virgin olive oil to taste
- 1 onion, thinly sliced
- 1 cup of potatoes
- ½ a cup of cherry tomatoes, quartered
- 3 bay leaves
- 1\4 cup of black olives, pitted
- 1 tbsp. grated grana cheese
- 2 tbsp. of breadcrumbs
- ½ cups of white wine
- Pepper to taste
- Salt to taste

Instructions:
Rinse the cod thoroughly and cut it into cubes.
Wash, peel, and cube the potatoes, soaking them in cold water for about 30 minutes.
In a bowl, combine the cherry tomatoes, sliced onion, pitted olives, and well-drained potatoes. Season with oil, salt, pepper, breadcrumbs, and grated Grana cheese. Mix well.
In an oiled baking dish, place the cod, add the vegetable mixture, and tuck in the bay leaves. Drizzle with additional oil and white wine.
Bake in the air fryer at 390°F for 40 minutes.

PESTO CHICKEN ROLLS

Servings: 2
Difficulty: Low
Cooking Time: 13 minutes

Ingredients:
- 6 chicken breast slices
- 6 tbsp of pesto
- 6 slices cooked ham
- 12 slices smoked scamorza cheese
- 5 fl oz beer
- Flour to taste
- Oil to taste
- Salt to taste

Instructions:
Lay the chicken slices on a flat surface and use a meat mallet to flatten them.
Spread one tablespoonof pesto on each slice, place a slice of ham, and add two slices of smoked scamorza cheese.
Roll up the chicken slices, coat them in flour, and secure them with toothpicks.
In a baking dish with some oil, brown the chicken rolls on the stove to seal the flavors.
Add the beer to the dish and bake in the fryer at 370°F for 13 minutes.

POLENTA BLOSSOMS WITH CREAMED COD

Servings: 2
Difficulty: Medium
Cooking Time: 20 minutes

Ingredients:
- For the Creamed Cod:
- 5.3 oz polenta
- 7 oz cod fillet (already soaked)
- Extra virgin olive oil
- 1\4 cups of milk
- 2.1 cups of water
- A small bunch of parsley
- Extra virgin olive oil
- Salt to taste
- Garlic powder to taste
- Pepper to taste

Instructions:
Begin by preparing the polenta. Bring water to a boil in a pot; add salt and a drizzle of oil. Gradually whisk in the polenta while boiling. Cook according to package instructions.
While the polenta is still hot, spread it on a parchment-lined baking tray to a thickness of about 0.8 inches. Let it cool.
In a saucepan, place the cod fillet pieces, cover with water, and bring to a boil. Drain and add milk. Cook until the cod softens and the milk reduces.
Allow the cod mixture to cool slightly, then blend with parsley, pepper, and garlic powder. Gradually add olive oil while blending. Adjust seasoning to taste.
Use a cookie cutter to shape the polenta into flowers. Spray both sides with oil and grill in the fryer at 390°F for ten minutes, turning halfway.
Serve the hot polenta blossoms with a quenelle of creamed cod on top.

POLENTA ROUNDS WITH LARDO AND ROSEMARY

Servings: 2
Difficulty: Medium
Cooking Time: 20 minutes

Ingredients:
- 5.3 oz polenta
- 5.3 oz Colonnata lardo
- 2 cups of water
- Extra virgin olive oil
- Rosemary
- Salt to taste

Instructions:
Begin by preparing the polenta following the instructions from the previous recipe.
Once the polenta has cooled, use a cookie cutter to create discs. Preheat the fryer to 390°F for three minutes. Place the polenta discs on the grill, spray both sides with oil, and grill at 390°F for ten minutes, turning halfway. Serve immediately, topping each disc with a slice of lardo and sprinkling rosemary needles.

POLENTA CUPS WITH SAUSAGE AND MUSHROOMS

Servings: 2
Difficulty: Medium
Cooking Time: 10 minutes

Ingredients:
- 5.3 oz polenta
- 1 garlic clove
- 10 cherry tomatoes
- 2 cups of water
- 1 tsp. of capers
- 1 bay leaf
- 7 oz sausage
- Grated cheese to taste
- ½ cup of Cardoncelli mushrooms
- Extra virgin olive oil
- Salt to taste

Instructions:
Begin by preparing the polenta following the instructions from previous recipes.
While the polenta is still hot, pour it into individual molds, pressing it against the sides to create a container shape.
Remove the casing from the sausage and crumble the meat. Sauté it in a pan with some oil and garlic. Add the mushrooms and cook for five minutes. Then, incorporate the bay leaf, capers, and tomatoes. Continue cooking for an additional ten minutes, adding water if necessary.
Fill each polenta cup with a generous spoonful of the filling and sprinkle with grated cheese.
Place the polenta cups on the grill and cook at 390°F for ten minutes.

BAKED SALMON AND ASPARAGUS

Servings: 2
Difficulty: Medium
Cooking Time: 17 minutes

Ingredients:
- 2 salmon fillets
- 12 asparagus
- 4 Tbsp. of soy sauce
- 1 Tbsp. of mustard
- Extra virgin olive oil
- Salt flakes

Instructions:
In a small dish, mix some oil, soy sauce, and mustard with a fork to blend. Marinate the salmon in this mixture for about an hour.
Place the salmon fillets on a baking tray lined with parchment paper, skin side down.
Clean the asparagus by peeling off the woody parts.
Arrange the asparagus next to the salmon, season with oil, and bake at 390°F for 17 minutes. Serve the asparagus sprinkled with salt flakes and drizzle with extra virgin olive oil.

SPINACINE (CHICKEN AND SPINACH PATTIES)

Servings: 2
Difficulty: Medium
Cooking Time: 13 minutes

Ingredients:
- 7 oz chicken breast
- 1 cup of spinach
- 1 egg
- 1 tbsp. of breadcrumbs
- 3 tbsp. of grated cheese
- 1 garlic clove
- Extra virgin olive oil
- Salt to taste
- Pepper to taste

For the Breading:
- 2 tbsp. of parmesan cheese
- 2 eggs
- Flour to taste
- Breadcrumbs to taste

Instructions:
In a pan, heat some oil with garlic. Add the spinach and cook on low heat with the lid on for five to six minutes. Remove the lid, let the liquid evaporate, season with salt, and remove the garlic. Let it cool.
In a blender, combine chicken, spinach, pepper, egg, breadcrumbs, and cheese. Blend. If the mixture is too soft, add more breadcrumbs. Form small balls and flatten them. Beat the eggs for bread with a pinch of salt.
In separate bowls, place some flour and a mixture of breadcrumbs and cheese. Coat the patties first in flour, then in egg, and finally in the breadcrumb mixture. Place them on parchment paper and refrigerate for about 30 minutes. Preheat the fryer to 390°F for three minutes, reduce to 370°F, and cook the patties for 13 minutes, spraying both sides with oil and turning them halfway through.

MORTADELLA MUFFINS

Servings: 8 muffins
Difficulty: Medium
Cooking Time: 17 minutes

Ingredients:
- 1 cup of flour
- 1\4 cup of milk
- 2 eggs
- 1\4 cup of sunflower seed oil
- 1.8 oz parmesan cheese
- 5.3 oz mortadella
- 1 packet of baking powder
- 4.2 oz provola cheese, cubed

Instructions:
In a mixer or bowl, combine flour, Parmesan, and baking powder.
Add eggs, oil, and milk while mixing.
Add the mortadella, finely chopped with a knife.
Pour the mixture into eight muffin cups, filling them ¾ full.
In each muffin cup, insert provola cheese cubes, pushing them into the batter. Bake at 370°F for 17 minutes. Check for doneness with a toothpick.

CHICKEN AND MORTADELLA CUTLETS

Servings: 2
Difficulty: Medium
Cooking Time: 16 minutes

Ingredients:
- 8 slices of chicken breast
- 8 slices of provolone cheese
- 4 slices of mortadella
- Extra virgin olive oil
- Salt, to taste
- Pepper, to taste

For the Breading:
- 2 eggs
- 2 tbsp. of grated cheese
- Breadcrumbs, to taste
- Flour, to taste

Instructions:
Flatten the chicken breast slices using a meat mallet or glass.
Place a slice of provolone and a slice of mortadella on four of the chicken slices. Cover with the remaining four chicken slices, pressing them lightly. Season both sides with salt and pepper.
Beat the eggs in a bowl with a pinch of salt. Prepare flour in a second bowl and a mixture of breadcrumbs and cheese in a third bowl.
Coat the cutlets first in flour, then in egg, and finally in breadcrumbs.
Spray both sides with oil and cook in the air fryer at 390°F for 16 minutes, turning halfway.

CHICKEN, MORTADELLA, AND PISTACHIO CUTLETS

Servings: 2
Difficulty: Medium
Cooking Time: 16 minutes

Ingredients:
- 8 slices of chicken breast
- 8 slices of provolone cheese
- 4 slices of mortadella
- Salt, to taste
- Pepper, to taste
- Extra virgin olive oil

For the Breading:
- 2 eggs
- 2 tbsp. of grated cheese
- 5 tbsp. of breadcrumbs
- 5 tbsp. of crushedpistachios
- Flour, to taste

Instructions:
Flatten the chicken breast slices using a meat mallet or glass.
Place a slice of mortadella and a slice of Emmental on four of the chicken slices. Cover with the remaining four chicken slices.
Season both sides with salt and pepper.
Beat the eggs in a bowl with a pinch of salt. Prepare flour in a second bowl, and a mixture of breadcrumbs, cheese, and crushed pistachios in a third bowl.
Coat the cutlets first in flour, then in egg, and finally in the breadcrumb-pistachio mixture. Spray both sides with oil and cook at 390°F for 16 minutes, turning halfway.

PROSCIUTTO ROLLS

Servings: 4
Difficulty: Medium
Cooking Time: 17 minutes

Ingredients:
- 1 cup of flour
- 2\3 cup of milk
- 1 tsp. dry yeast
- 1\8 cup of butter
- 5.3 oz cooked ham
- 1 tbsp sugar
- 5.3 oz cheese
- Salt to taste

Instructions:
In a bowl, place the flour. Dissolve the yeast and sugar in the milk and add it to the flour. Add butter and knead until smooth. Let it rise, covered until doubled in size.
Finely chop the ham and cheese.
Roll out the dough on a lightly floured surface and cut it into 4x4-inch squares. Fill with ham and cheese, roll them up, and seal the ends. Let them rise for another hour.
Preheat the air fryer to 360°F for three minutes. Brush with milk and bake for two minutes at 360°F, then reduce to 320°F and bake for another 15 minutes.

WURSTEL ROLLS

Servings: 4
Difficulty: Medium
Cooking Time: 13 minutes

Ingredients:
- 1 cup of flour
- 2\3 cup of milk
- 1 tsp. of dry yeast
- 1\8 cup of butter
- 3 large packs of wurstels
- 1 tbsp of sugar
- Salt to taste

Instructions:
Follow the same procedure as the Prosciutto Rolls, but instead of ham and cheese, wrap the dough around the wurstels. Bake at 360°F for 13 minutes. Serve with your preferred sauces, such as mayonnaise or mustard.

BREADED AND FRIED EGGPLANTS

Servings: 2
Difficulty: Medium
Cooking Time: 15 minutes

Ingredients:
- 2 eggplants
- Breadcrumbs, to taste
- 1 egg
- 2 tbsp. of grated parmesan cheese
- Flour, to taste
- Salt, to taste

Instructions:
Slice the eggplants into 0.2-inch thick slices. Salt them and let them drain in a colander for 30 minutes to release water. Dredge the eggplant slices in flour, then dip in the beaten egg, and finally coat with a mixture of breadcrumbs and cheese. Spray both sides with oil and cook at 360°F for 15 minutes, turning halfway and spraying the other side with oil.

RUSTIC FLUTE WITH MUSHROOMS AND SAUSAGE

Servings: 2
Difficulty: Medium
Cooking Time: 15 minutes

Ingredients:
- 1 rectangular puff pastry sheet
- 1 cup of mixed mushrooms
- 7 oz sausage
- 1\4 cup of white wine
- 4.4 oz mozzarella cheese
- 1 garlic clove
- Extra virgin olive oil
- Salt, to taste

Instructions:
In a pan with oil and garlic, sauté the crumbled sausage. Add the mushrooms, deglaze with wine, and cook covered for 5 minutes.
Remove the garlic, season with salt, and let it cool.
Chop the mozzarella.
Cut the pastry into four pieces and make horizontal cuts on half of the right side, stopping 0.4 inches from the edge. Place the mushroom and sausage mixture and chopped mozzarella on the uncut side. Seal the edges well. Bake at 356°F for ten minutes.

SHRIMP WITH BELL PEPPERS

Servings: 2
Difficulty: Medium
Cooking Time: 15 minutes

Ingredients:
- 8 large shrimp
- 1 bell pepper
- Extra virgin olive oil
- 1 onion
- Salt and pepper, to taste

Instructions:
Wash the bell pepper, remove the seeds, and slice it. Peel the onion and combine it with the bell pepper in a bowl. Season with oil, salt, and pepper.
Add the cleaned shrimp and marinate for 30 minutes.
Transfer everything to a baking dish and bake in the air fryer at 360°F for 15 minutes, stirring occasionally.

BREADED SHRIMP

Servings: 2
Difficulty: Medium
Cooking Time: 10 minutes

Ingredients:
- 17.6 oz shrimp
- 1 tbsp. of grated parmesan cheese
- 1\3 cup of breadcrumbs
- Extra virgin olive oil
- Herbs, to taste
- Salt and pepper, to taste

Instructions:
In a freezer bag, combine the washed and cleaned shrimp with salt, oil, pepper, and finely chopped herbs. Shake well to mix.
Add breadcrumbs and cheese to the bag. Place the shrimp on the air fryer grill, spray with oil, and cook at 340°F for ten minutes.

BREADED COD

Servings: 2
Difficulty: Medium
Cooking Time: 20 minutes

Ingredients:
- 14.1 oz cod
- Extra virgin olive oil
- Herbs, to taste
- Breadcrumbs, to taste

Instructions:
Check the cod fillets for bones and, if necessary, remove them with tweezers.
Cut the cod into rectangles measuring 3.1 x 1.2 inches.
In a bowl, prepare a mixture of breadcrumbs and finely chopped herbs.
Coat the cod in the mixture, spray with oil, and grill at 390°F for 20 minutes, turning halfway. Adjust the cooking time if the fillet is thinner or the pieces are smaller.

COD AND SPECK

Servings: 2
Difficulty: Medium
Cooking Time: 15 minutes

Ingredients:
- 10.6 oz cod
- 3.5 oz speck (smoked ham)

Instructions:
Check the cod fillets for bones and, if necessary, remove them with tweezers.
Cut the cod into rectangles. Wrap each cod fillet with a slice of speck.
Grill in the air fryer at 374°F for 15 minutes, turning halfway. Thinner fillets are recommended for optimal results.

PUMPKIN AND SPECK

Servings: 2
Difficulty: Medium
Cooking Time: 25 minutes

Ingredients:
- 1 1\2 cups of pumpkin
- 5.3 oz smoked bacon slices
- Oil spray

Instructions:
Peel the pumpkin, remove seeds and fibers, and slice it into pieces about 0.4 inches thick.
Wrap bacon slices around the pumpkin slices, spray with oil, and bake at 360°F for 25 minutes.

SMOKED SCAMORZA CHEESE AND SPECK

Servings: 2
Difficulty: Medium
Cooking Time: 8 minutes

Ingredients:
- 6 smoked scamorza cheeses
- 6 slices of speck (smoked ham)

Instructions:
Wrap each scamorza cheese with a slice of speck.
Arrange them in a baking dish and bake in the air fryer at 390°F for eight minutes.

SWORDFISH WITH CRUNCHY COATING

Servings: 4
Difficulty: Medium
Cooking Time: 25 minutes

Ingredients:
- 4 swordfish steaks
- 1 garlic clove
- 1 tbsp. of chopped pistachios
- Olive oil, to taste
- A bunch of parsley
- A bunch of chives
- 2.8 oz breadcrumbs
- 1 lemon

Instructions:
Toast the breadcrumbs in a pan with a little oil.
Wash and chop the parsley, chives, and garlic, placing them on a plate.
Add the toasted breadcrumbs, pistachio crumbs, and grated lemon zest to the plate.
Mix everything and coat the fish steaks with the breadcrumb mixture, placing them on the grill. Spray with oil and cook at 390°F for 20 minutes, turning and spraying halfway through.

PUMPKIN, MUSHROOMS, AND POTATOES RECIPE

Servings: 2
Difficulty: Medium
Cooking Time: 40 minutes

Ingredients:
- 1 1\3 cups of pumpkin
- 3\4 cup of mushrooms
- 2 sprigs of thyme
- 2 potatoes
- 1 onion
- Extra virgin olive oil
- Salt, to taste

Instructions:
Peel and cube the potatoes; wash and drain them. Peel the pumpkin, remove seeds and fibers, then cut into cubes. Peel and slice the onion.
Combine everything in a large bowl and season with oil, salt, and thyme. Mix to coat everything and transfer to a baking dish. Bake at 360°F for 25 minutes.
Meanwhile, clean the mushrooms, slice them, and add them to the baking dish, continuing to cook for another 15 minutes. If necessary, add some water to prevent them from drying out too much.

ZUCCHINI AND CHERRY TOMATOES

Servings: 2
Difficulty: Medium
Cooking Time: 20 minutes

Ingredients:
- 2 zucchinis
- Extra virgin olive oil
- 1 garlic clove
- 6 ripe cherry tomatoes
- 1 bay leaf
- Salt, to taste

Instructions:
Wash the zucchinis, trim the ends, and slice them into pieces about 0.12-0.16 inches thick.
Finely chop the garlic and add it to a baking dish with a generous amount of oil.
Add the zucchini slices, quartered cherry tomatoes, and bay leaf.
Mix and cook at 360°F for 20 minutes, stirring occasionally.

"SCRAMBLED" ZUCCHINI

Servings: 2
Difficulty: Medium
Cooking Time: 20 minutes

Ingredients:
- 2 zucchinis
- 1 garlic clove
- Extra virgin olive oil
- 1 bay leaf
- 3 ripe cherry tomatoes
- 2 eggs
- Salt, to taste

Instructions:
Wash the zucchinis, trim the ends, and slice them into pieces about 0.12-0.16 inches thick.
Finely chop the garlic and add it to a baking dish with a generous amount of oil. Preheat the air fryer to 370°F for two minutes.
Add the zucchini slices, bay leaf, and quartered cherry tomatoes. Mix and cook at 360°F for 15 minutes, stirring occasionally. Break the eggs, beat them with a pinch of salt, and add them to the zucchini, stirring to "scramble" them. Add a little water and continue cooking for another five minutes.

SAUSAGE AND ZUCCHINI

Servings: 2
Difficulty: Medium
Cooking Time: 25 minutes

Ingredients:
- 2 zucchinis
- 10.6 oz sausage
- 1 garlic clove
- Extra virgin olive oil
- A bunch of parsley
- Salt, to taste

Instructions:
Wash the zucchinis, trim the ends, and slice them into approximately 0.2-inch thick pieces.
Season with oil, garlic, and finely chopped parsley, and salt.
Cut the sausage into small pieces and place them in a baking dish. Cook at 370°F for about 20-25 minutes.

MUSHROOMS AND SAUSAGE

Servings: 2
Difficulty: Medium
Cooking Time: 25 minutes

Ingredients:
- 3\4 cup of champignon mushrooms
- 1 garlic clove
- 10.6 oz sausage
- A bunch of parsley
- Extra virgin olive oil
- 2 tbsp. of white wine
- Salt, to taste

Instructions:
Cut the sausage into small pieces and place it in a baking dish, setting the air fryer to 370°F for about 15 minutes. Finely chop the garlic, clove, and parsley. Clean the mushrooms, slice them, add the chopped mixture, and season with a drizzle of oil. Combine the mushrooms with the sausage, pour in the wine, and continue cooking for another ten minutes, stirring occasionally. Adjust with salt and serve.

FETA ON PARCHMENT PAPER

Servings: 2
Difficulty: Medium
Cooking Time: 10 minutes

Ingredients:
- 7 oz Feta cheese
- ½ Red bell pepper
- Yellow and red cherry tomatoes
- Oregano
- Black olives
- Extra virgin olive oil

Instructions:
Wash and slice the bell pepper. Season with oil and oregano. Add olives and quartered tomatoes. Mix everything and let it marinate for about 30 minutes.
Cut a piece of parchment paper and spread half of the tomatoes on it. Place the feta on top, cover with the remaining tomatoes, and seal the parchment paper.
Cook at 360°F for ten minutes. Serve directly in the parchment paper, drizzling with fresh olive oil.

FETA ON PARCHMENT PAPER WITH CARAMELIZED ONIONS

Servings: 2
Difficulty: Medium
Cooking Time: 10 minutes

Ingredients:
- 7 oz Feta cheese
- 1 tbsp. of sugar
- 2 red onions
- 1 1\2 fl oz vinegar

Instructions:
Peel and slice the onions. Place them on a parchment paper, drizzle with oil, and add sugar and vinegar. Mix everything and seal the parchment paper with the closure facing down.
Cook at 360°F for 15 minutes until the onions are soft.
Cut a piece of parchment paper and place half of the caramelized onions at the bottom. Put the feta on top and cover with the remaining onions. Seal the parchment paper and cook at 360°F for ten minutes. Serve with toasted bread slices.

PARMIGIANA TOWERS

Servings: 2
Difficulty: Medium
Cooking Time: 10 minutes

Ingredients:
- 2 small eggplants
- 5 red cherry tomatoes
- 5 yellow cherry tomatoes
- Extra virgin olive oil
- 2 basil leaves
- 1 mozzarella
- Salt, to taste

For the Basil and Almond Sauce:
- 1 bunch of basil
- 1 garlic clove
- 1 oz pecorino cheese
- 1 oz grated parmesan cheese
- 1\3 cup of extra virgin olive oil
- 10 almonds

Instructions:
Prepare the sauce by placing basil, garlic, cheese, almonds, and oil in a blender. Blend intermittently to avoid heating the blades. Adjust with salt and set aside.
Wash and quarter the tomatoes. Season with salt, oil, and torn basil leaves. Allow them to marinate for about 30 minutes.
Wash, trim, and slice the eggplants. Spray them with oil on both sides and cook at 360°F for ten minutes, turning halfway. Once cooked, season with salt and a drizzle of oil. Slice the mozzarella and let it drain.
Assemble the parmigiana tower by placing two slices of eggplant at the base of the plates. Add a slice of mozzarella, some tomatoes, a few drops of basil sauce, and continue for three layers. Finish the last layer with tomatoes and some basil sauce. Decorate the plate with the sauce.

STUFFED ARTICHOKES IN THE AIR FRYER

Servings: 2
Difficulty: Medium
Cooking Time: 20 minutes

Ingredients:
- 6 artichokes
- 1 stale bread roll
- ½ onion
- 1.8 oz grated parmesan cheese
- ½ carrot
- 1 oz breadcrumbs
- 1 bunch of parsley
- ½ celery stalk
- 1 potato
- Garlic powder
- 2 eggs
- 1 lemon
- Pepper, to taste
- Salt, to taste

Instructions:
Start by preparing the broth. In a pot, add water, onion, carrot, celery, parsley, and diced potato.
Clean the artichokes by removing the tough outer leaves, trimming the tops, and peeling the stems. Cut them so they can stand upright. Dice the remaining artichoke parts and stems, keeping them in a bowl with water and lemon juice. Blanch the artichokes in boiling water for about ten minutes to soften them. Drain and let them cool.
Soak the stale bread in water, squeeze out the excess water, and combine it in a bowl with eggs, cheese, breadcrumbs, salt, pepper, garlic powder, and finely chopped parsley. Mix to form a dough.
Fill each artichoke with the bread mixture and place them in a baking dish. Add a ladle of broth and cook at 360°F for 20 minutes. Occasionally check and add more broth if needed.

VEAL ROLLS WITH PEAS AND CARROTS

Servings: 2
Difficulty: Medium
Cooking Time: 26 minutes

Ingredients:
- 6 veal slices
- 1 small onion
- 3 slices of cooked ham
- Extra virgin olive oil
- 6 slices of Fontina cheese
- 1 bunch of parsley
- 4\5 cup of peas
- 1\4 cup of white wine
- 2 carrots
- Flour, to taste

Instructions:
Lay out the veal slices and fill each with ham and cheese. Roll them up and secure them with toothpicks. Dredge the rolls in flour, shaking off the excess.
In a baking dish with a drizzle of oil, place the veal rolls and brown at 360°F for six minutes, turning to seal all sides. Meanwhile, peel and chop the onion and carrots. Add them to the meat along with the peas. Pour in the wine, add some water, and cook at 360°F for 20 minutes.

VEAL SCALOPPINE WITH MUSHROOMS

Servings: 2
Difficulty: Medium
Cooking Time: 24 minutes

Ingredients:
- 6 veal slices (from the loin)
- 1 cup of champignon mushrooms
- 1 carrot
- 1\8 cup of white wine
- 1 garlic clove
- Extra virgin olive oil
- 1 knob of butter
- 1 bunch of parsley
- Pepper, to taste
- Flour, to taste
- Salt, to taste

Instructions:
Coat the veal slices in flour and place them in a baking dish with a drizzle of oil. Bake in the air fryer at 360°F for six minutes on each side until a crust forms.
Remove the meat from the dish and add butter, sliced champignon mushrooms, chopped carrot, garlic, and parsley. Cook at 350°F for ten minutes, adding wine and stirring occasionally.
Reintroduce the scaloppine to the mushrooms, season with salt and pepper, and continue cooking at 350°F for eight minutes, turning the meat halfway through.

CHICKEN SCALOPPINE WITH LEMON

Servings: 2
Difficulty: Medium
Cooking Time: 16 minutes

Ingredients:
- 6 chicken breast slices
- Extra virgin olive oil
- 1 bunch of parsley
- 1 knob of butter
- 2 small lemons
- Flour, to taste
- Pepper, to taste
- Salt, to taste

Instructions:
Coat the chicken slices in flour and place them in a baking dish with a drizzle of olive oil and butter. Bake at 360°F for six minutes on each side until a crust forms. Season with salt and pepper.
Squeeze the lemons and add the juice to the meat. Continue cooking for an additional ten minutes, turning the meat halfway through. If necessary, add a small amount of water to create a sauce.
Before serving, garnish with chopped parsley.

CITRUS TURKEY BREAST

Servings: 2
Difficulty: Medium
Cooking Time: 24 minutes

Ingredients:
- 6 turkey breast slices
- Extra virgin olive oil
- 1 small lemon
- 1 knob of butter
- ½ red orange
- ¼ pink grapefruit
- Flour, to taste
- Pepper, to taste
- Salt, to taste

Instructions:
Coat the turkey slices in flour and place them in a baking dish with a drizzle of olive oil and butter. Bake in the air fryer at 360°F for seven minutes on each side until a crust forms. Season with salt.
Squeeze the citrus fruits and add the juice to the meat. Continue cooking for an additional ten minutes, turning the slices halfway through. Sprinkle fresh pepper before serving.

CAULIFLOWER BOWLS PIZZAIOLA STYLE

Servings: 2
Difficulty: Medium
Cooking Time: 16 minutes

Ingredients:
- 1 cup of cauliflower
- 1 oz grated Parmesan cheese
- 3.5 oz Emmental cheese
- 10 black olives
- 6 slices of bread (pan carré)
- Garlic powder, to taste
- ½ cup of tomato pulp
- A pinch of oregano
- Extra virgin olive oil
- Pepper, to taste
- Salt, to taste

Instructions:
Clean the cauliflower and create florets. Blanch them in salted water, then drain, finely chop, and sauté in a pan with a drizzle of oil. Add the tomato pulp and oregano, letting it simmer. Allow it to cool.
Slice the olives and dice the Emmental cheese. Combine them with the cauliflower, add Parmesan cheese, and mix well. Spray the bread slices with oil and season both sides with salt, pepper, and garlic powder. Press each slice into a muffin tin to form a bowl shape. Bake in the air fryer at 370°F for six minutes.
Fill the bread bowls with the cauliflower mixture and bake at 370°F for five minutes, allowing the cheese to melt.

AIR FRYER ROASTED MACKEREL

Servings: 2
Difficulty: Medium
Cooking Time: 15 minutes

Ingredients:
- 2 mackerels, approximately 5.3 oz each
- Extra virgin olive oil

Instructions:
Clean the fish by removing the innards and thoroughly rinse them.
Place a perforated parchment paper on the air fryer grill, position the fish on it, and cook at 360°F for 15 minutes, flipping halfway through. Adjust cooking times based on the fish size.
Serve with a drizzle of raw olive oil. Optionally, enhance with freshly ground pepper, garlic, a few drops of lemon juice, and chopped parsley.

POTATO AND CHEESE PUFF PASTRY

Serving Size: 2
Difficulty: Medium
Cooking Time: 35 minutes

Ingredients:
- 1 round puff pastry roll
- 1 egg
- 1 potato
- 2 tbsp. of parmesan cheese
- 3.5 oz ricotta cheese
- 5 slices of smoked scamorza cheese
- 3 slices of cooked ham
- Pepper
- Salt

Instructions:
Allow the puff pastry to sit at room temperature for approximately ten minutes, then unroll it and line the pan with it. Peel the potato and thinly slice it using a mandolin. Rinse and soak the slices in cold water.
In a bowl, combine ricotta with salt, pepper, and egg. Spread this mixture over the puff pastry. Layer with cheese slices and ham slices.
Drain the potato slices and season with oil, salt, and pepper. Arrange the potato slices over the ham, overlapping them. Fold the edges of the puff pastry.
Bake covered with parchment paper at 370°F for 20 minutes. Remove the parchment paper and continue baking for an additional 15 minutes.

ROASTED ARTICHOKES

Servings: 2
Difficulty: Medium
Cooking Time: 20 minutes

Ingredients:
- 3 artichokes
- Lemon water
- Olive oil
- Salt, to taste
- Pepper, to taste

Instructions:
Clean the artichokes by removing the tougher leaves and halving them, eliminating the choke if present. Immediately soak them in lemon water to prevent browning.
Rinse the artichokes and gently open them with your hands. Season with olive oil, salt, and pepper. Roast at 370°F for 20 minutes. Serve with an additional drizzle of olive oil.

GRATINATED ARTICHOKES

Servings: 2
Difficulty: Medium
Cooking Time: 25 minutes

Ingredients:
- 3 artichokes
- 1 bunch of parsley
- 2 tbsp. of parmesan cheese
- 3 tbsp. of breadcrumbs
- Extra virgin olive oil
- Salt, to taste
- 1 garlic clove
- Pepper, to taste

Instructions:
Clean the artichokes by removing the tougher leaves and halving them, eliminating the choke if present. Immediately soak them in lemon water to prevent browning.
In a bowl, combine breadcrumbs, Parmesan, salt, and pepper. Finely chop garlic and parsley, adding them to the breadcrumb mixture. Incorporate a drizzle of oil while mixing to create crumbs.
Drain the artichokes and gently open them with your hands. Drizzle with oil and generously coat with the breadcrumb mixture. Bake at 360°F for 20-25 minutes.

CAULIFLOWER AND POTATO GRATIN

Servings: 2
Difficulty: Moderate
Cooking Time: 30 minutes

Ingredients:
- 1 cup of cauliflower
- 1.8 oz parmesan cheese
- 3 potatoes
- 1\4 cup of breadcrumbs
- 1 bunch of parsley
- Extra virgin olive oil
- 3 eggs
- 1 slice of speck, 0.2 in- thick
- 5.3 oz scamorza cheese
- 7 oz mozzarella cheese
- Salt, to taste
- Pepper, to taste

Instructions:
Clean the cauliflower and cut it into florets. Peel and dice the potatoes. Boil the vegetables for approximately 15 minutes until they are softened but not fully cooked. Drain and transfer them to a bowl. Add olive oil, salt, and pepper. Mix well and allow it to cool.
In the meantime, dice the mozzarella and scamorza cheese and cut the speck into small pieces. Once the vegetables have cooled, incorporate eggs, mozzarella, scamorza, and speck.
Pour the mixture into a baking dish, sprinkle with breadcrumbs and Parmesan, and bake at 390°F for 15 minutes.

MARINATED SALMON

Servings: 2
Difficulty: Moderate
Cooking Time: 15 minutes

Ingredients:
- 4 pieces of salmon fillets
- 1 bunch of chives
- 1 lemon
- 1 garlic clove
- 2 tbsp. of extra virgin olive oil
- 1 tsp. of paprika
- Salt, to taste
- Pepper, to taste

Instructions:
Combine lemon juice, extra virgin olive oil, paprika, finely chopped chives, salt, and pepper in a bowl to create the marinade.
Integrate the crushed garlic clove into the mixture.
Submerge the salmon fillets in the marinade, ensuring they are thoroughly coated.
Preheat the air fryer and lightly coat it with oil spray. Place the marinated salmon fillets inside.
Cook at 360°F for approximately 15 minutes or until the salmon reaches a tender and slightly golden consistency.

BONUS EXTRA!!

SCAN THE QR CODE TO UNLOCK 100+ BONUS AIR FRYER DESSERT RECIPES AND GET ACCESS TO NEW VIDEO RECIPES EVERY MONTH!

SCAN ME

Index

Air Fryer Roasted Mackerel	104
Almond-Crusted Umbrina	80
Aromatized Salted Chicken	89
Artichoke Flans with Gorgonzola Sauce	15
Baked Cod with Potatoes and Olives	94
Baked Fusilli with Asparagus and Speck	59
Baked Lasagna with "Fried" Eggplant	50
Baked Nests	57
Baked Pennette with Speck and Zucchini	59
Baked Ricotta	30
Baked Salmon and Asparagus	96
Baked Tomato and Mozzarella Calzones	22
Baked Wheat	58
Beef Tagliata	85
Beer-Marinated Chicken	88
Bell Pepper Boats with Tuna	66
Bread and Mortadella Balls	81
Bread Bowls with Spicy Marinated Shrimp in Mango Sauce	74
Breaded and Fried Eggplants	98
Breaded Bread	13
Breaded Chicken Wings	79
Breaded Cod	99
Breaded Mozzarella Balls	29
Breaded Pork Steaks	75
Breaded Shrimp	99
Breaded Vegetable Sticks	9
Breaded Zucchini with Ham and Galbanino	39
Bread Meatballs	21
Bread Meatball-Stuffed Tomatoes	52
Bread Spirals with Mortadella and Provolone	36
Bresaola, Arugula, and Grana Bagels	22
Brise Tart with Eggplant and Sausage	45
Bruschetta with Eggplant Cream	28
Bruschetta with Eggs and Avocado	25
Bruschetta with Grilled Zucchini, Avocado, and Sesame Tuna	24
Bruschetta with Robiola, Figs and Prosciutto Crudo	25
Bruschetta with Stracchino Cheese and Sausage	25
Bruschetta with Stracciatella, Mortadella, and Pistachios	25
Bucatini Puttanesca	62
Caprese Crumble	31
Cauliflower and Potato Gratin	106
Cauliflower Bowls Pizzaiola Style	104
Cauliflower Gratin	43
Cauliflower Gratin Pie	61
Cereal Breadsticks	34
Cereal Bread with Melting Filling	41
Cheese-Crusted Bread Rolls	33
Chicken and Mortadella Cutlets	97
Chicken Braciolette	67
Chicken Bundles with Speck and Scamorza	65
Chicken Drumsticks with Tzatziki Sauce	76
Chicken Legs with Speck	85
Chicken, Mortadella, and Pistachio Cutlets	97
Chicken Parcels with Spices	80
Chicken Roll in Puff Pastry	92
Chicken Rolls with Ham and Cheese	78
Chicken Roll with Potatoes	78
Chicken Scaloppine with Lemon	103
Chicken Tagliata with Valerian, Almonds, Mango, and Avocado	80
Chicken Wings with Potatoes in Sauce	66
Chili Pepper Bread Cubes	14
Citrus-Infused Salt-Baked Chicken	87
Citrus-Marinated Salmon	87
Citrus Turkey Breast	104
Classic Baked Pasta	54
Classic Panzerotti	37
Cod and Speck	99
Cod Fillet Marinated in Yogurt and Breaded	69
Colorful Cereal Bruschetta	24
Conchiglioni with Ricotta and Ham	56
Crispy Bacon, Scrambled Eggs, and Toasted Bread	26
Crostini with Friggitelli and Cherry Tomatoes	16
Cuttlefish and Squid Burger	77
Cuttlefish Steak	89
Eggplant Brise Tart	45
Eggplant "Bruschetta"	13
Eggplant Cubes	28
Eggplant Cutlet	13
Eggplant Meatballs	21
Eggplant Parmigiana	84

Eggplants and Cherry Tomatoes	27
Eggs with Zucchini	81
Fake Eggplant Bruschetta with Ham and Mozzarella	31
Fake Pumpkin Omelette	42
Fan Eggplants	28
Farmer's Eggs	81
Feta on Parchment Paper	101
Feta on Parchment Paper with Caramelized Onions	102
FIRST COURSES	48
Flavored Mixed Vegetables	9
Fried Calamari	74
"Fried" Ricotta	11
"Fried" Zucchini Flowers in Batter	20
Friggitelli with Coarse Salt	16
Gorgonzola and Caramelized Onion Baskets	44
Gorgonzola and Walnut Panzerotti	37
Gratinated Artichokes	105
Gratinated Melting Cake	30
Gratinated Onion	38
Gratinated Scallops	76
Gratinated Swordfish	71
Gratinated Tomatoes	30
Gratin Scallops	83
Green Bean Salad with Soft-Boiled Eggs	18
Grilled Eggplants	10
Grilled Zucchinis	10
Ham and Cheese Toast	24
Ham and Mozzarella Quiche	19
Hamburger	65
Ham, Cheese, Zucchini, and Pesto Toast	24
Ham Panfocaccia	40
Italian-style Tomatoes	35
Lamb Chops	90
Lasagna with Gorgonzola and Walnuts	57
Lasagna with Porcini Mushrooms	60
Lasagna with Zucchini, Shrimp, and Pistachio Crumble	60
Lemon-Scented Egg Salad	18
Lime and Pink Pepper Chips (San Carlo Style)	23
Macaroni with Béchamel and Pecorino	55
Macaroni with Broccoli, Cauliflower, and Gratin	51
Macaroni with Cauliflower and Bacon	51
Marinated Chicken Breast with Avocado and Lamb's Lettuce	73
Marinated Chicken Thighs with Yogurt	68
Marinated Salmon	106
Marinated Squid	76
Marinated Turkey	82
Mc-Style Fries	26
Meat and Spinach Frittata	71
Meatballs	68
Meatballs in Bacon	75
Meat Flan	79
Meat Skewers with Vegetables	91
Melting Rice Frittata	49
Melting Wheat	58
Milk Bread Rolls	36
Minted Zucchini	47
Mixed Baked Vegetables	30
Mortadella and Pistachio Ground Meat Roll	86
Mortadella and Provolone Pie	61
Mortadella Muffins	96
Mozzarella in Carrozza	10
Muffins with Zucchini and Sun-Dried Tomatoes	14
Mushroom and Ham Panzerotti	38
Mushroom and Pumpkin Lasagna	57
Mushroom and Sausage Crepes	49
Mushrooms and Sausage	101
Mushrooms Stuffed with Bread	72
New Potatoes	36
Olive Bread Rolls	35
Omelette	26
Onion and Gorgonzola Quiche	19
Onion and Olive Spirals	11
Onion Bread Roses	35
Onion Rings in Batter	26
Orange Glazed Salmon	83
Orecchiette with Tomato and Mozzarella Gratin	52
Oven-Baked Lasagna with Cacio e Pepe	63
Oven-Baked Pumpkin Lasagna	63
Panfocaccia with Mortadella and Spicy Provolone	40
Paprika Chicken Thighs	68
Parmesan Biscuits	34
Parmigiana Towers	102
Penne with Artichokes and Sausage	50
Penne with Chicken and Bell Peppers	50
Penne with Guanciale and Walnuts	62
Penne with Spinach Sauce in Parchment	55
Pesto Chicken Rolls	94
Pistachio-Crusted Scallops	84
Pizzaiola Biscuits	33
Polenta Blossoms with Creamed Cod	95

Polenta Cups with Sausage and Mushrooms	95	Pancarrè	82
Polenta Rounds with Lardo and Rosemary	95	Rosemary Bread Cubes	13
Pork Capocollo Gratin	85	Rosemary-infused Pork Ribs	83
Pork Tenderloin in Crust	67	Rosemary-Infused Salt-Baked Chicken	87
Potato and Caciocavallo Cheese Meatballs	32	Rose Puff Pastry Cake	38
Potato and Cheese Puff Pastry	105	Rustic Flute with Mushrooms and Sausage	98
Potato Croquettes	23	Rustic Potato, Mushroom, and Speck Galette	33
Potato Cubes with Oregano and Garlic	39	Salami Ring Cake Without Leavening	46
Potatoes and Bacon	79	Salmon and Avocado Bagels	21
Potatoes and Rosemary	44	Salmon and Potato Bake	93
Potatoes Pizzaiola Style	43	Salmon and Robiola Pasta Bake	62
Potatoes with Gorgonzola, Speck, and Walnuts	44	Salmon, Cherry Tomato, and Arugula Bread Bowls	92
Potatoes with Stracchino Cheese and Mortadella	43	Salmon Fillet in Parchment	71
Potato Frittata	27	Salmon Fillet with Pistachio Crust	69
Potato Millefeuille with Speck and Smoked Scamorza 23		Salmon Pastry Parcels	93
Potato Nests with Mushrooms and Sausage	91	Salt-Baked Chicken	87
Pouches of Scamorza Cheese with Speck and Walnuts 74		Salt-Baked Sea Bream	88
		Sausage and Zucchini	101
Prosciutto Rolls	97	Sausage, Bacon, and Zucchini Rolls	91
Puff Pastry Cones with Cheese Cream	18	Savory Baskets Filled with Bresaola and Avocado	70
Puff Pastry Grissini with Speck and Cheese	16	Savory Baskets Filled with Shrimp	69
Puff Pastry Rustic with Stewed Turnip Tops	15	Savory Cake with Mushrooms, Potatoes, Speck, and Brie	42
Puff Pastry with Cabbage, Sausage, and Cheese	70	"Scrambled" Zucchini	101
Puff Pastry with Ricotta and Salmon	40	Seafood Burger with Swordfish, Salmon, and Squid	78
Pumpkin and Cheese Crumble	31	Seafood Cartocci	61
Pumpkin and Speck	99	SECOND COURSES	64
Pumpkin Chips	20	Sesame Breaded Chicken	65
	39	Shrimp with Bell Peppers	98
Pumpkin Lasagna	56	Smoked Scamorza Cheese and Speck	99
Pumpkin, Mushrooms, and Potatoes Recipe	100	Speck-Wrapped Scallops	84
Pumpkin Savory Cake	45	Spinach Croquettes with Melting Heart	17
Quiche	27	Spinach Medallions	15
Quick Stuffed Danube	46	Spinach-Stuffed Ground Meat Roll	86
Rice Croquettes	29	Spinacine (Chicken and Spinach Patties)	96
Rice Croquettes with Melting Heart	29	Spring Rolls	16
Rice-Stuffed Tomatoes	52	Squid and Peas	89
Rice with Potatoes and Mussels	54	STARTERS	8
Rigatoni Pie	60	Strozzapreti with Speck and Walnuts	59
Roast Beef with Vegetable Sauce	65	Stuffed Artichokes in the Air Fryer	102
Roasted Artichokes	105	Stuffed Bell Peppers with Meat	66
Roasted Chestnuts	39	Stuffed Bell Peppers with Ricotta and Spinach	92
Roasted Chicken	88	Stuffed Bread Rolls	41
Roasted Pepper Crostini	9	Stuffed Mushrooms with Meat	73
Roasted Pumpkin	20	Stuffed Potatoes with Tuna	67
Rolls with Zucchini, Speck, and Philadelphia on		Stuffed Turkey Rolls	93

Dish	Page
Stuffed Zucchini with Rice	53
Super Pizzaiola Chicken with Roasted Potatoes	86
Surprise Tomatoes	22
Swordfish Meatballs	73
Swordfish Skewers with Pistachio Sauce and Caramelized Onions	77
Swordfish with Crunchy Coating	100
Tomato and Mozzarella Rustic	17
Tomini with Mortadella and Pistachio Crust	70
Tomini with Walnuts and Dried Figs	14
Tomini Wrapped in Bacon	14
Tortelloni with Burrata and Basil on Eggplant Cream	56
Tortiglioni with Melted Cheese and Vegetables	55
Triangular Pastries with Turnip Greens, Onion, and Grana Cheese	41
Trofiette with Pumpkin Cream	51
Tuna and Zucchini Patties	32
Tuna Stuffed Eggs	72
Turkey Rolls with Asparagus and Speck	94
Turkey Roll with Vegetables	75
Umbrina (Meagre) with Sun-Dried Tomatoes, Pistachio Crust, and Zucchini Pesto	77
Veal Rolls with Mortadella and Provolone Cheese	90
Veal Rolls with Peas and Carrots	103
Veal Rolls with Peas in White Sauce	90
Veal Scaloppine with Mushrooms	103
Vegetable Ring Cake Without Leavening	46
Wheat with Cardoncelli Mushrooms and Cherry Tomatoes	58
Whole Wheat Bread with Walnuts	34
Wurstel Rolls	98
Wurstel Rustic	17
Zucchini and Cherry Tomatoes	100
Zucchini and Robiola Rolls	19
Zucchini and Sausage Skewers	72
Zucchini Flowers with Ricotta and Mint	12
Zucchini Flowers with Smoked Cheese and Ham	12
Zucchini Frittata	11
Zucchini Rolls Caprese Style	42
Zucchini Rolls with Ham and Mozzarella	12
Zucchini Rolls with Philadelphia and Salmon	32
Zucchini with Couscous and Shrimp	53
Zucchini with Ricotta and Basil	82

Made in the USA
Las Vegas, NV
14 June 2024